By

© Copyright 2015

Disclaimer

The information provided in this book is designed to provide helpful information on the subjects discussed. The author's books are only meant to provide the reader with the basics knowledge of a certain topic, without any warranties regarding whether the student will, or will not, be able to incorporate and apply all the information provided. Although the writer will make his best effort share his insights, learning is a difficult task and each person needs a different timeframe to fully incorporate a new topic. This book, nor any of the author's books constitute a promise that the reader will learn a certain topic within a certain timeframe.

LEARN HTML IN A DAY

The Ultimate Crash Course to Learning the Basics of HTML in No Time

Table of Contents

Exercises

Chapter 6: Forms

Creating a Form with The <form> element

The action attribute

The method attribute

The id attribute

The name attribute

The enctype attribute

The accept-charset attribute

The novalidate attribute

The target attribute

The autocomplete attribute

Form Controls

Text Inputs

Using placeholders to Illustrate Example Input

Ensuring User Privacy and Security with the autocomplete Attribute

Ensuring information is Provided with the required Attribute

Buttons

Creating Buttons Using the <input> element

Creating Buttons Using the <button> element

Check Boxes

Radio Buttons

Select Boxes

The <select> element

The <option> Element

Creating Scrolling Select Boxes

Selecting Multiple Options with the multiple Attribute

Introduction

Hello and thank you for choosing this book to guide you on your journey towards learning HTML! HTML is the language of the web, as virtually all webpages are written in this markup language, so you are on the right path towards learning to build amazing websites. This book will thoroughly guide you through the main components of HTML documents and how to use them effectively. The book is organized in chapters that revolve around a main topic. Each chapter contains code examples with explanations to strengthen your knowledge. At the end of each chapter there are a number of exercises for you to test the knowledge of the chapter. The answers for those can be found at the back of the book. So, without further ado, let's dive right into learning HTML.

Chapter 1: Structuring Pages

Structured Documents

Every day, you come across all kinds of printed documents — newspapers, train timetables, and insurance forms. You can think of the web as being a sea of documents that all link together and bear a strong similarity to the printed documents that you meet in everyday life.

Take the example of a newspaper. A newspaper consists of several stories or articles (and probably a fair smattering of advertisements, too). Each story has a headline and then some paragraphs, perhaps a subheading, and then some more paragraphs; it may also include a picture or two.

The structure of articles on news websites is similar to the structure of articles in newspapers. Each article consists of headings, paragraphs of text, and some pictures. (Sometimes the pictures might be replaced by a video.) The parallel is quite clear; the only difference is that in a newspaper you may have several stories on a single page, whereas on the web each story tends to get its own page. The news websites also often use homepages that display the headline and a brief summary of the stories.

Consider another example: You're catching a train to see a friend, so you check the schedule or timetable to see what time the train leaves. The main part of the schedule is a *table* telling you what times trains arrive and when they depart from different stations. You can probably think of several types of documents that use tables. From the listings in the financial supplement of your paper to the TV schedule, you come across tables of information every day — and often when this information is put on the web, these tables are re-created.

Another common type of printed document is a *form*. For example, think about a common form from an insurance company. Such a form contains fields to write your name, address, and the amount of coverage, along with check boxes to indicate the number of rooms in the house and what type of lock is on the front door. There are lots of forms on the web, from simple search boxes that ask what you are looking for to the registration forms you are required to fill out before you can place an online order for books or CDs.

As you can see, there are many parallels between the structure of printed documents you come across every day and pages you see on the web. When you are writing web pages, it is the HTML code you start learning in this chapter that tells the web browser how the information you want to display is structured — what text to put in a heading, paragraph, or table, and so on so that the browser can present it properly to the user.

HTML5

Even if you have never seen any HyperText Markup Language (HTML) code, you may know that it is used to create web pages. There have been five versions of HTML since the web began, and the development of the language is overseen by an organization called the World Wide Web Consortium (W3C).

This book focuses on the latest version of the language, popularly referred to as HTML5. There are two other versions you might encounter. These are HTML 4.01, the last major version of the language from December 1999, and a stricter version from 2000 called Extensible HyperText Markup Language (XHTML). XHTML is still popular in some applications, so important differences between it and HTML5 will be called out in the text.

As its name suggests, HTML is a markup language, which may sound complicated until you realize that you come across markup every day. When creating a document in a word processor, you can add styles to the text to explain the document's structure. For example, you can distinguish headings from the main body of the text using a heading style (usually with a larger font). You can use the Return (or Enter) key to start a new paragraph. You can insert tables into your document to hold data or create bulleted lists for a series of related points, and so on. Although this does affect the presentation of the document, the key purpose of this kind of markup is to provide a structure that makes the document easier to understand.

When marking up documents for the web, you perform a similar process, except you do it by adding things called tags to the text. With HTML, the key thing to remember is that you must add the tags to indicate the structure of the document (not how you want it to be presented); for example, which part of the document is a heading, which parts are paragraphs, what belongs in a table, and so on. Browsers such as Internet Explorer, Firefox, and Google Chrome all use this markup to help present the text in a familiar fashion, similar to that of a word processor — main headings are bigger than the text in paragraphs, there is space above and below each paragraph, and lists of bullet points have a circle in front of them.

You don't need any special programs to write web pages; you can simply use a text editor such as Notepad on Windows or TextEdit on a Mac and save your files with the .html or .htm file extension. Let's look at an example page:

```
<html>
    <head>
        <title>Popular Websites: Google</title>
    </head>
    <body>
        <h1>About Google</h1>
        <p>Google is best known for its search
        engine, although Google now offers a number
        of other services.</p>
        <p>Google's mission is to organize the
        world's information and make it universally
        accessible and useful.</p>
        <p>Its founders Larry Page and Sergey Brin
        started Google at Stanford University.</p>
    </body>
</html>
```

This may look a bit confusing at first, but it will all make sense soon. As you can see, there are several sets of angle brackets with words or letters between them, such as `<html>`, `<head>`, `</title>`, and `</body>`. These angle brackets and the words inside them are known as tags, and these are the markup previously mentioned. You can save this file as a .html file and open it in any browser of our choice.

To understand the markup in this first example, you need to look at what is written between the angle brackets and compare that with what you see in the figure, which is what you do next.

Tags and Elements

If you look at the first and last lines of the code for the previous example, you see pairs of angle brackets containing the letters "html". Starting on the first line, the first angled bracket looks like a less-than sign (<); then there are the letters "html," followed by a second angled bracket, which looks like a greater-than sign (>). The two brackets and all the characters between them are known as a *tag*.

In this example, there are lots of tags, and they are all in pairs; there are *opening* tags and *closing* tags. The closing tag is always slightly different from the opening tag in that it has a forward slash (/) after the first angled bracket: </html>.

A pair of tags and the content these include are known as an element.

The opening tag says, "This is the beginning of a heading" and the closing tag says, "This is the end of a heading." Like most tags in HTML, the text inside the angled brackets explains the purpose of the tag—here `h1` indicates that it is a level 1 heading (or top-level heading). As you will see shortly, there are also tags for subheadings (`<h2>`, `<h3>`, `<h4>`, `<h5>`, and `<h6>`). If you don't put tags around the words "About Google," it is just another bit of text; it would not be clear that these words formed the heading.

Now look at the three paragraphs of text about the company; each one is placed between an opening `<p>` tag and a closing `</p>` tag. And you guessed it, the p stands for paragraph.

WARNING You must understand the basic distinction between tags and elements: A tag usually consists of left-angle and right-angle brackets and letters and numbers between those brackets, whereas elements are the opening and closing tags plus anything between the two tags.

WARNING To be precise, there are also tags that consist of just one left-angle bracket and one right-angle bracket, with no content and no closing tag. These are also elements.

As you can see, the tags throughout this example actually describe what you will find between them, creating the structure of the document. The text between the `<h1>` and `</h1>` tags is a heading, and the text between the opening `<p>` and closing `</p>` tags makes up paragraphs. Indeed, the whole document is contained between opening `<html>` and closing `</html>` tags.

You often find that terms from a family tree are used to describe the relationships between elements.

For example, an element that contains another element is known as the parent, whereas the element that's between the parent element's opening and closing tags is called a child of that element. So, the `<title>` element is a child of the `<head>` element, the `<head>` element is the parent of the `<title>` element, and so on. Furthermore, the `<title>` element can be thought of as a grandchild of the `<html>` element.

Additionally, if two elements are children of the same parent, they are referred to as siblings.

It is worth noting that the tags in this example are all in lowercase characters; you sometimes see web pages written in HTML where tags are uppercase (or a mix of uppercase and lowercase letters). When XHTML was introduced, with its stricter rules, it stated that all tags were written in lowercase. Technically, HTML5 loosens these restrictions to enable mixed case. In practice you generally see lowercase even in HTML5 documents.

NOTE Even though HTML5 enables mixed case tags, lowercase should be used for consistency with XHTML documents, which require lowercase tags.

Separating Heads from Bodies

Whenever you write a web page in HTML, the whole of the page is contained between the opening <html> and closing </html> tags, just as it was in the previous example. Inside the <html> element, there are two main parts to the page:

- The <head> element: Often referred to as the head of the page, this contains information about the page. (This is not the main content of the page.) For example, it might contain a title and a description of the page or instructions on where a browser can find CSS rules that explain how the document should look. It consists of the opening <head> tag, the closing </head> tag, and everything in between.

- The <body> element: Often referred to as the body of the page, this contains the information you actually see in the main browser window. It consists of the opening <body> tag, the closing </body> tag, and everything in between.

Together, the <html>, <head>, and <body> elements make up the skeleton of an HTML document— they are the foundation upon which every web page is built. Inside the <head> element of the first example page, you see a <title> element:

```
<head>
     <title>Popular Websites: Google</title>
</head>
```

Between the opening `<title>` tag and the closing `</title>` tag are the words "Popular Websites: Google," or the title of this web page. Opening a browser shows the words at the top of the browser window, which is where browsers such as Internet Explorer, Firefox, and Chrome display the title of a document. It is also the name they use when you save a page in your Favorites List, and it helps search engines understand what your page is about. The `<title>` element is mandatory for all web pages. The real content of your page is held in the `<body>` element, which is what you want users to read, and this is shown in the main browser window.

WARNING The \<head\> element contains information about the document, which is not displayed within the main page. The \<body\> element holds the actual content of the page viewed in your browser.

You may have noticed that the tags in this example appear in a symmetrical order. If you want to have one element inside another, both the element's opening and closing tags must be inside the containing element. For example, the following is allowed:

```
<p> This paragraph contains some <em>emphasized
text.</em></p>
whereas the following is wrong because the closing
</em> tag is not inside the paragraph element:
<p> This paragraph contains some <em>emphasized text.
</p></em>
```

In other words, if an element is to contain another element, it must wholly contain that element. This is referred to as nesting your elements correctly.

Attributes Tell You about elements

Attributes in HTML are much like the attributes you experience every day. They are the qualities that describe a person or thing, such as a tall man or a brown dog. Similarly, HTML elements can be described in ways that web browsers can understand. This section looks at attributes, starting with the most important one that beats at the heart of the web. What differentiates web documents from standard documents are the links (or hyperlinks) that take you from one web page to another. Look at a link by adding one to the example you just looked at. Links are created using an <a> element. (The a stands for anchor.)

You can add a link from this page to Google in a new paragraph at the end of the document. There is just one new line in this example and that line is highlighted:

```
<html>
      <head>
            <title>Popular Websites: Google</title>
      </head>
      <body>
            <h1>About Google</h1>
            <p>Google is best known for its search
            engine, although Google now offers a number
            of other services.</p>
            <p>Google's mission is to organize the
            world's information and make it
            universally accessible and useful.</p>
            <p>Its founders Larry Page and Sergey Brin
            started Google at Stanford University.</p>
            <p><a href="http://www.Google.com/">Click
            here to visit Google's Web    site.</a></p>
      </body>
</html>
```

Inside this new paragraph is the <a> element that creates the link. Between the opening <a> tag and the closing </a> tag is the text that you can click, which says, "Click here to visit Google's Web site." Opening the file in a browser shows you what this page looks like in a browser. If you look closely at the opening tag of the link, it carries something called an attribute. In this case, it's the href attribute; this is followed by an equal sign and then a pair of quotation marks, which contain the URL for Google's website. In this case, the href attribute tells you where the link should take you. You look at links in greater detail in the Chapter 3, "Links and Navigation," but for the moment this illustrates the purpose of attributes.

- Attributes are used to say something about the element that carries them, and they always appear on the opening tag of the element that carries them. Almost all attributes consist of two parts: a name and a value. The name is the property of the element that you want to set. In this example, the <a> element carries an attribute whose name is href, which you can use to indicate where the link should take you.

- The value is what you want the value of the property to be. In this example, the value was the URL of the site that the link should take you to, so the value of the href attribute is http://www.google.com.

The value of the attribute should always be put in double quotation marks and separated from the name with the equal sign.

There are several attributes in HTML5 that do not consist of a name/value pair but consist of just a name. These are called boolean attributes and you will learn more about those in the section "Attribute Groups."

Another common attribute on anchors is the title attribute, which gives a plain language description of the target of the link. You could add one to the example to inform people that Google is a popular search engine.

```
<a href="http://www.Google.com"    title="Google.com is
the world's most popular search engine">
```

This illustrates that elements can carry several attributes; although, an element should never have two attributes of the same name.

Attributes

As you have seen, attributes live on the opening tag of an element and provide extra information about the element that carries them. Many attributes consist of a name and a value; the name reflects a property of the element the attribute describes, and the value is a value for that property. For example, the lang attribute describes the language used within that element; a value such as EN-US would indicate that the language used inside the element is U.S. English.

Some attributes consist of only a name, such as required or checked. These are called boolean attributes. To say something is a boolean is to indicate that it can be in one of two states: true or false. For HTML attributes the presence of one of the boolean attributes in a tag indicates that the value is true. So, the following are equivalent:

```
<input type="text" required >
<input type="text" required="true">
```

Many of the elements in HTML can carry some or all the attributes you will meet in this section. At first some of them may sound a little abstract; although, they will make more sense as you see them used throughout the book. So don't worry if they do not make much sense at first. In this section, you look at three groups of attributes common to many HTML elements:

- Core attributes: Including the class, id, style, and title attributes

- Internationalization attributes: For example, the dir and lang attributes

- Accessibility attributes: For example, accesskey and tabindex

WARNING Together, the core attributes and the internationalization attributes are known as universal attributes.

Core attributes

The four core attributes that you can use on the majority of HTML elements (although not all) are:

```
id title class style
```

Throughout the rest of the book, these attributes are revisited when they have special meaning for an element that differs from the description given here; otherwise their use can generally be described as you see in the subsections that follow.

The id Attribute

You can use the id attribute to uniquely identify any element within a page. You might want to uniquely identify an element so that you can link to that specific part in the document or to specify that a CSS style or piece of JavaScript should apply to the content of just that one element within the document. The syntax for the id attribute is as follows (where string is your chosen value for the attribute):

```
id="string"
```

For example, you can use the id attribute to distinguish between two paragraph elements, like so:

```
<p id="accounts">This paragraph explains the role of
```

```
the accounts department.</p>
<p id="sales">This paragraph explains the role of the
sales department.</p>
```

Following are some special rules for the value of the id attribute:

- Must begin with a letter (A–Z or a–z) and can then be followed by any number of letters, digits (0–9), hyphens, underscores, colons, and periods. (You may not start the value with a digit, hyphen, underscore, colon, or period.)

- Must remain unique within that document; no two id attributes may have the same value within one HTML page. This case should be handled by the class attribute.

The class Attribute

You can use the class attribute to specify that an element belongs to a class of elements. For example, you might have a document that contains many paragraphs, and a few of those paragraphs might contain a summary of key points, in which case you could add a class attribute whose value is summary to the relevant <p> elements to differentiate those paragraphs from the rest in the document.

```
<p class="summary">Summary goes here</p>
```

It is commonly used with CSS. The syntax of the class attribute is as follows:

```
class="className"
```

The value of the attribute may also be a space-separated list of class names, for example:

```
class="className1 className2 className3"
```

The title Attribute

The title attribute gives a suggested title for the element. The syntax for the title attribute is as follows:

```
title="string"
```

The behaviour of this attribute depends upon the element that carries it; although, it is often displayed as a tooltip or while the element loads. Not every element that can carry a title attribute actually needs one, so when you meet an element that particularly benefits from use of this attribute, you will see the behaviour it has when used with that element.

The style Attribute

The style attribute enables you to specify CSS rules within the element. You meet CSS later, but for now, here is an example of how it might be used:

```
<p style="font-family:arial; color:#FF0000;">Some
text.</p>
```

As a general rule, however, it is best to avoid the use of this attribute. If you want to use CSS rules to govern how an element appears, it is better to use a separate style sheet instead. The only place where this attribute is still commonly used is when it is set with JavaScript.

Internationalization

The web is a worldwide phenomenon. Because of this, there are mechanisms built into the tools that drive the web that allow authors to create documents in different languages. This process is called internationalization. Two common internationalization attributes help users write pages for different languages and character sets:

```
dir lang
```

You look at each next, but it is worth noting that even in current browsers, support for these attributes is still patchy. Therefore where possible you should specify a character set that creates text in the direction you require. The website of a helpful W3C document that describes internationalization issues in greater detail is found at www.w3.org/TR/i18n-html-tech-char/; although, you briefly look at each of these attributes next.

NOTE The internationalization attributes are sometimes referred to as the i18n attributes, an odd name that comes from the draft-ietf-html-i18n specification in which they were first defined.

The dir Attribute

The dir attribute enables you to indicate to the browser the direction in which the text should flow: left to right or right to left.

When you want to indicate the directionality of a whole document (or the majority of the document), use it with the `<html>` element rather than the `<body>` element for two reasons: Its use on the <HTML> element has better support in browsers, and it can apply to the header elements as well as those in the body. You can also use the dir attribute on elements within the body of the document if you want to change the direction of a small portion of the document. The dir attribute can take one of two values, as you can see in the table.

Value	Meaning
ltr	Left to right (this is set by default)
rtl	Right to left (for languages such as Hebrew or Arabic that are read right to left)

The lang Attribute

The lang attribute enables you to indicate the main language used in a document.
The lang attribute was designed to offer language-specific display to users; although, it has little effect in the main browsers.
The benefits of using the lang attribute are for search engines (which can tell the user which language the document is authored in), screen readers (which might need to pronounce different languages in different ways), and applications (which can alert users when either they do not support that language or it is a different language than their default language).

When used with the `<html>` element, the attribute applies to the whole document; although, you can use it on other elements, in which case it just applies to the content of those elements. The values of the lang attribute are ISO-639-1 standard two-character language codes. If you want to specify a dialect of the language, you can follow the language code with a dash and a subcode name. Table 1-2 offers some examples.

Value	Meaning
ar	Arabic
en	English
en-us	US English
zh	Chinese

Core Elements

Now take a closer look at the four main elements that form the basic structure of every document: `<html>`, `<head>`, `<title>`, and `<body>`. These four elements should appear in every HTML document that you write, and you will see them referred to throughout this book as the skeleton of the document.

About DOCTYPEs

Although the four main elements describe the skeleton of a document, one final piece qualifies the document as a whole. The DOCTYPE (for DOCument TYPE) tells the browser what rules to follow when showing the document to the user. These rules are called modes.

This book focuses on the HTML5 DOCTYPE that puts the browser into strict mode. You can think of strict mode as the browser acknowledging the author wanting to play by the rules. The other common mode, quirks mode, tells the browser you will use some funky rules, which have their origins in the late 1990s. You don't want to have anything to do with quirks mode. So what does the HTML5 DOCTYPE look like?

```
<!doctype html>
```

Start all your documents with that DOCTYPE, and your pages will always render in the correct mode. The basic skeleton of an HTML5 page therefore looks like this:

```
<!doctype html>
<html>
    <head>
        <title>The Skeleton of an HTML5
Document</title>
    </head>
    <body>
    </body>
</html>
```

The <html> element

The <html> element is the containing element for the whole HTML document. After the DOCTYPE declaration, each HTML document should have an opening <html> tag, and each document should end with a closing </html> tag. The <html> element can also carry the following attributes, which you learned about in the "Attribute Groups" section:

```
id dir lang
```

The \<head> element

The `<head>` element is just a container for all other header elements. It is the first thing to appear after the opening `<html>` tag.

Each `<head>` element should contain a `<title>` element indicating the title of the document; although, it may also contain any combination of the following elements, in any order:

- `<base>`, which you will meet in Chapter 3, "Links and Navigation";
- `<link>` to link to an external file, such as a style sheet;
- `<style>` to include CSS rules inside the document;
- `<script>` for including script in the document;
- `<meta>`, which includes information about the document such as a description or the name of the author

The opening `<head>` tag can carry the following attributes:

```
id dir lang
```

The \<title> element

You should specify a title for every page that you write using the `<title>` element (which, as you saw earlier in the chapter, is a child of the `<head>` element). It is presented and used in several ways:

- At the top of a browser window (as you saw in the first example)
- As the default name for a bookmark in browsers such as IE, Firefox, and Chrome
- By search engines that use its content to help index pages

Therefore, you must use a title that describes the content of your site. For example, the homepage of this book should not just say "Homepage"; rather it should describe what your site is about. Rather than just saying "HTML Homepage," it is more helpful to write:

```
<title>HTML: Programming Books, Learn HTML Fast and
Easy </title>
```

The test for a good title is whether visitors can tell what they will find on that page just by reading the title, without looking at the actual content of the page, and whether it uses words that people would use if they were going to search for this kind of information.

The `<title>` element should contain only the text for the title; it may not contain any other elements. The `<title>` element can carry the following attributes:

```
id dir lang
```

Links and Style Sheets

Although you'll learn more about CSS and JavaScript at some other point, they are going to be a common element on every page you look at and build, so it's important that we quickly cover how to include them in your web pages. Adding a style sheet relies on the `<link>` element. The `<link>` element also uses the `href` attribute, which you learned about already, to point to a resource on the web. In this case, instead of pointing to a new page or website to visit when a link is clicked, it points to the location of a file containing style information for the current page. The `rel` (for relation) attribute indicates that the linked document is a style sheet and should be handled accordingly.

```
<link rel="stylesheet" href="css/main.css">
```

Adding a script to the page is even easier. You add a
`<script>` element to the page and add a `src` attribute
pointing to the location of the JavaScript file you want to use.

```
<script src="js/main.js"></script>
```

WARNING *Always include the closing* **</script>** *tag when
inserting a script element, even if, as in this case, there's no
content between the opening and closing tags. If you don't,
strange things can happen.*

You need to start using one piece of JavaScript. Now that you
know how to add a script to the page, you're ready to learn
about the HTML5 Shiv and Modernizr.

Ensuring Backward Compatibility for HTML5 Tags

There's one final element you see in many HTML5
documents. Because of a wrinkle in the way that Internet
Explorer deals with unknown HTML elements, you need to
include a small piece of JavaScript in the head of your
document. If you don't, things look wrong when you view
your pages in Internet Explorer 8 or less. It's called the
HTML5 Shiv, and including it in your pages looks something
like this:

```
<script
src="http://cdnjs.cloudflare.com/ajax/libs/html5shiv/3.
6/html5shiv.min.js"> </script>
```

As for what it does, for the time being, just know that it needs to be there, or you'll get unpredictable results in IE8 and older. If you're interested in the history of this small but vitally important script, see Paul Irish's article, "The History of the HTML5 Shiv," at `http://paulirish.com/2011/the-history-of-the-html5-shiv/`. Building on the HTML5 Shiv, there's another library you'll encounter in this book. It's called Modernizr and at its core includes the HTML5 Shiv for backward compatibility; in addition, it adds in tests for emerging web features that you can use when building sites. That way you can ensure that you're not trying to serve something to a browser that can't actually handle it. You'll learn about Modernizr throughout the book, but for now the following code sample shows how to include Modernizr:

```
<script
src="http://cdnjs.cloudflare.com/ajax/libs/modernizr/2.
6.1/modernizr.min.js"> </script>
```

The power of Modernizr will become more apparent throughout the book. For now the examples in the book use the simpler HTML5 Shiv to ensure compatibility with Internet Explorer 8 and below. And now, with that trip through the head, you're ready to start adding in the star of the show, the content of your page.

The <body> element

The `<body>` element appears after the `<head>` element, and as you have already seen, it contains the part of the web page that you actually see in the main browser window, which is sometimes referred to as *body content*. The `<body>` element can carry all the attributes from the *attribute groups*.

Common Content elements

You spend most of the remaining part of this chapter learning the different elements you can use to describe the structure of text. These include:

- The six levels of headings: `<h1>`, `<h2>`, `<h3>`, `<h4>`, `<h5>`, and `<h6>`
- Paragraphs `<p>`, preformatted sections `<pre>`, line breaks `<br />`, and addresses `<address>`
- Grouping elements: `<div>`, `<header>`, `<hgroup>`, `<nav>`, `<section>`, `<article>`, and `<hr>`
- Presentational elements: `<b>`, `<i>`, `<sup>`, and `<sub>`
- Phrase elements: `<em>`, `<strong>`, `<abbr>`, `<dfn>`, `<blockquote>`, `<q>`, `<cite>`, `<code>`, `<kbd>`, `<var>`, and `<samp>`
- Lists such as unordered lists using `<ul>` and `<li>`; ordered lists using `<ol>` and `<li>`; and definition lists using `<dl>`, `<dt>`, and `<dd>`
- Editing elements: `<ins>` and `<del>`

That may sound like a lot of elements, but you might be surprised at how quickly you can move through them.

Basic text formatting

Because almost every document you create contains some form of text, the elements you are about to meet are likely to feature in most pages that you will build. In this section, you learn how to use *basic text formatting elements:*

- `<h1>`, `<h2>`, `<h3>`, `<h4>`, `<h5>`, and `<h6>`
- `<p>`, `<br>`, and `<pre>`

As you read through this section, one browser might display each of these elements in a certain way, and another browser might display the same page in a slightly different way. For example, the typefaces used, the font sizes, and the spaces around these elements may differ between browsers. (And therefore the amount of space a section of text takes up can vary, too.) Before you look at the elements, it helps to know how text displays by default without any elements. This helps demonstrate the importance to use markup to tell the browser if you want it to treat text differently.

White Space and Flow

Before you start to mark up your text, it's best to understand what HTML does when it comes across spaces and how browsers treat long sentences and paragraphs of text. You might think that if you put several consecutive spaces between two words, the spaces would appear between those words onscreen, but this is not the case; by default, only one space displays. This is known as *white space collapsing*. Similarly, if you start a new line in your source document, or you have consecutive empty lines, these will be ignored and simply treated as one space, as will tab characters. For example, consider the following paragraph:

```
<p>This    paragraph shows how   multiple spaces
between      words are treated as a single space. This
is known as white space collapsing, and the big spaces
between     some of the   words will not appear    in
the browser.            It also demonstrates how the
browser will treat multiple carriage returns (new
lines) as a single space, too.</p>
```

The browser treats the multiple spaces and several carriage returns (where text appears on a new line) as if there were only one single space. It also enables the line to take up the full width of the browser window.

Now look at the code for this example again, and compare where each new line starts in the code with where each new line starts onscreen. Unless told otherwise, when a browser displays text, it automatically takes up the full width of the screen and wraps the text onto new lines when it runs out of space. You can see the effect of this better if you open this example in a browser and try resizing the browser window (making it smaller and larger) and notice how the text wraps at new places on the screen.

White space collapsing can be particularly helpful because it enables you to add extra spaces into your HTML that do not show up when viewed in a browser. You can use these spaces to indent your code, which makes it easier to read. The first two examples in this chapter demonstrated indented code, where child elements are indented from the left to distinguish them from their parent elements, which is used this throughout this book to make the code more readable. (If you want to preserve the spaces in a document, you need to use either the <pre> element, which you learn about later in the chapter, or an entity reference such as , a nonbreaking space). Now that you know how multiple spaces and line breaks are collapsed, you can see why you must learn how to use the elements in the rest of this chapter to break up and control the presentation of your text.

Creating Headings using <hn> elements

No matter what sort of document you create, most documents have headings in one form or another. Newspapers use headlines; a heading on a form tells you the purpose of the form; the title of a table of sports results tells you the league or division the teams play in; and so on.

In longer pieces of text, headings can also help structure a document. If you look at the table of contents for this book, you can see how different levels of headings have been arranged to add structure to the book, with subheadings under the main headings.

HTML offers six levels of headings, which use the elements <h1>, <h2>, <h3>, <h4>, <h5>, and <h6>. Browsers display the <h1> element as the largest of the six and <h6> as the smallest. You can open a sample file in your browser to see what these headings will look like. We will do this in a bit.

WARNING Most browsers display the contents of the <h1>, <h2>, and <h3> elements larger than the default size of text in the document. The content of the <h4> element would be the same size as the default text, and the content of the <h5> and <h6> elements would be smaller unless you instruct them otherwise using CSS.

Here is another example of how you might use headings to structure a document, where the <h2> elements are subheadings of the <h1> element. (This actually models the structure of this section of the chapter.)

```
<h1>Basic Text Formatting</h1>
<p> This section is going to address the way in which
you mark up text. Almost every document you create will
contain some form of text, so this will be a very
important section. </p>
<h2>White Space and Flow</h2>
<p> Before you start to mark up your text, it is best
to understand what HTML does when it comes across
spaces and how browsers treat long sentences and
paragraphs of text.</p>
<h2>Creating Headings</h2>
<p> No matter what sort of document you are creating,
most documents have headings in some form or
other...</p>
```

The six heading elements can all carry the universal attributes:

```
class id style title dir lang
```

Creating paragraphs using the <p> element

The <p> element offers another way to structure your text. Each paragraph of text should go in between an opening <p> and closing </p> tag, as in this example:

```
<p>Here is a paragraph of text.</p>
<p>Here is a second paragraph of text.</p>
<p>Here is a third paragraph of text.</p>
```

When a browser displays a paragraph, it usually inserts a new line before the next paragraph and adds a little bit of extra vertical space.
The <p> element can carry all the universal attributes:

```
class id style title dir lang
```

Creating Line Breaks using the <br> element

Whenever you use the <br> element, anything following it starts on the next line. The <br> element is an example of an *empty element*; you don't need opening and closing tags, because there is nothing to go in between them.

You can use multiple <br> elements to push text down several lines, and many designers use two line breaks between paragraphs of text rather than using the <p> element to structure text, as follows:

```
Paragraph one<br><br>
Paragraph two<br><br>
Paragraph three<br><br>
```

Although two <br> elements look similar to using a <p> element, remember that HTML markup is supposed to describe the structure of the content. So if you use two <br> elements between paragraphs, you are not describing the document structure.

NOTE Strictly speaking, do not use <br> elements to position text; use them only within a block-level element. The <p> element is a block-level element; you learn more about these in the "Understanding Block and Inline Elements" section.

Here you can see an example of the <br> element in use within a paragraph:

```
<p>When you want to start a new line you can use the
line break element. So, the next<br />word will appear
on a new line.</p>
```

The <br> element can carry the following attributes:

```
class id style title
```

Creating preformatted Text using the <pre> element

Sometimes you want your text to follow the exact format of how it is written in the HTML document; you don't want the text to wrap onto a new line when it reaches the edge of the browser. You also don't want it to ignore multiple spaces, and you want the line breaks where you put them.

Any text between the opening <pre> tag and the closing </pre> tag preserves the formatting of the source document. You should be aware, however, that most browsers display this text in a monospaced font by default. (Courier is an example of a monospaced font because each letter of the alphabet takes up the same width. Compare this to a nonmonospaced font, where an *i* is usually narrower than an *m*.)

The most common uses of the <pre> element are to represent computer source code. For example, the following shows some JavaScript inside a <pre> element:

```
<pre>
function testFunction( strText ){
      console.log( strText )
}
</pre>
```

Opening the following code in a browser shows how the content of the <pre> element displays in the monospaced font. More important, you can see how it follows the formatting shown inside the <pre> element—the white space is preserved.

Although tab characters can have an effect inside a <pre> element, and a tab is supposed to represent eight spaces, the implementation of tabs varies across browsers, so it is advisable to use spaces instead. You will come across more elements that you can use to represent code in the next chapter, "Finetuning Your Text," which covers the <code>, <kbd>, and <var> elements.

Block vs. Inline

Now that you have seen many of the elements that you can use to mark-up text, you must consider all the elements that live inside the `<body>` element because each can fall into one of two categories:

- Block-level elements
- Inline elements

This is quite a conceptual distinction, but it has important ramifications for other features of HTML.

Block-level elements appear on the screen as if they have a carriage return or line break before and after them. For example, the `<p>`, `<h1>`, `<h2>`, `<h3>`, `<h4>`, `<h5>`, `<h6>`, `<ul>`, `<ol>`, `<dl>`, `<pre>`, `<hr />`, `<blockquote>`, and `<address>` elements are all block-level elements. They all start on their own new lines, and anything that follows them appears on its own new line, too.

Inline elements, on the other hand, can appear within sentences and do not need to appear on new lines of their own. The `<b>`, `<i>`, `<u>`, `<em>`, `<strong>`, `<sup>`, `<sub>`, `<small>`, `<ins>`, `<del>`, `<code>`, `<cite>`, `<dfn>`, `<kbd>`, and `<var>` elements are all inline elements.

For example, look at the following heading and paragraph; both of these elements start on new lines, and anything that follows them goes on a new line, too. Meanwhile, the inline elements in the paragraph are not placed on their own new lines. Here is the code:

```
<h1>Block-Level Elements</h1>  <p><strong>Block-level
elements</strong> always start on a new line. The
<code>&lt;h1&gt;</code> and <code>&lt;p&gt;</code>
elements will not sit  on the same line, whereas the
inline elements flow with the rest of the  text.</p>
```

You can see what this looks like in a browser.

Strictly speaking, inline elements may not contain block-level elements and can appear only within block-level elements. (So you should not have a <b> element outside a block-level element.) Block-level elements, meanwhile, can contain other block-level elements and inline elements.

Content grouping

You can find one of the most interesting new additions to the HTML5 specification in a number of new elements added to aid in grouping content. As you just learned, elements represent the different parts of an article with different levels of headings and paragraphs. As you'll learn throughout the chapter, there are many other elements left to mark up to describe text.

One thing that was lacking was the ability to group all that well-described content into meaningful ways. So, although you could write an article and mark up each paragraph meaningfully, it wasn't possible to indicate that the entire block of text was an article. HTML5 changes that with the addition of several new elements designed to enable you to more accurately group content. This section introduces the various ways to group content in HTML.

The new outline algorithm in HTML5

In adding these new grouping elements, the authors of the specification made a change to the way headings are used in HTML. Before HTML5, the general standard was to have one <h1> element per page. The basic idea was that the entire HTML document was by itself a standalone element and should therefore have just one overall outline with a single <h1> at the top of the tree.

As the web evolved to contain more complicated, compound documents, this concept no longer held true for many of the documents on the web. With a blog, you can easily have several separate articles all contained in a single HTML document. Each of those articles could contain a logical outline of its own, independent of the rest of the page. Because of this, the ability to add more than one <h1> to the page inside different sectioning elements was added.

As you'll learn throughout this section and as you continue to work with HTML5, there's much greater flexibility in the ways you can structure pages using the new mark-up.

As an aid to work with HTML5 documents, there's a handy bookmarklet and Google Chrome extension called the HTML5 Outliner (h5o) that can help to analyze the structure of your pages. Even experienced authors find it useful, so it's definitely good to have on hand to make sure your pages make sense at the outline level. You can download it from Google code: http://code.google.com/p/h5o/.

The <div> element

Before the extension of the grouping elements in HTML5, the most common container for groups of HTML elements was the <div>. It represents a generic block of content and is designed to be used with classes and ids to give structure to documents. Taking the mark-up from Example Café, you could mark it up with <div> elements representing different content sections.

For example, if you want to set the header apart in some way, you can mark it up like the following example. Using a <div> with a class of header you can encapsulate the site title and tagline into a single structure:

```
<div class="header">  <h1>EXAMPLE CAFE</h1>  <p>Welcome
to example cafe. We will be developing this site
throughout the book.</p> </div>
```

Although this is actually quite useful for styling and scripting, there's no semantic meaning behind the <div>, no matter how well chosen the classes or ids are. As you see throughout this section, the new sectioning elements in HTML5 enhance the utility of the <div> with (mostly) straightforward semantic meaning.

The <header> element

As part of the development of the new specification, the editor of the HTML standard, Ian Hickson, did a survey of the web and identified common mark-up patterns. Some of these he captured as new HTML elements. This is one such element.

As you saw in the previous example, the concept of a "header" for common introductory or navigation content is a useful one and was repeated over and over on the web. Marking up the previous example with a <header> simplifies the mark-up and imparts more semantic meaning to the page.

```
<header>  <h1>EXAMPLE CAFE</h1>  <p>Welcome to example
cafe. We will be developing this site throughout the
book.</p> </header>
```

Although this example shows a header generated at the page level, you can also use headers within other grouping elements. For example, an <article> element, which you'll learn about shortly, can have its own header containing information about the author, the data published, and the title of the article.

The <hgroup> element

The <hgroup> element is designed to group together multiple levels of headings that have some logical connection, for example, subheadings, alternative titles, or taglines. Adding an <hgroup> element, and a silly tagline, to the previous example illustrates how to use the <hgroup> element:

```
<header>  <hgroup>     <h1>EXAMPLE CAFE</h1>
<h2>Serving Home Style Example Markup since 2012</h2>
</hgroup> </header>
```

The <nav> element

The <nav> element represents a navigation section of the page, containing a list of links to other pages or site sections within the site or application. Because the Example Café site is going to have more than one page, look at one way to mark up a simple menu linking to other pages on the site. In this example you can see a series of <p> tags, containing links to the site's other pages. Later you learn about working with lists and learn a more common pattern for marking up navigational elements. For now, just focus on the use of the <nav> element.

```
<nav>
     <p><a href="recipes.html">Recipes</p>
     <p><a href="menu.html">Menu</a></p>
     <p><a href="opening_times.html">Opening
Times</a></p>
     <p><a href-"contact.html">contact</a></p>
</nav>
```

The <section> element

The `<section>` element is used to represent a section of a document or application. A `<section>` differs from a `<div>`, the most generic content grouping element, by the idea that content contained in a `<section>` is designed to be part of the document's outline.

Although the Example Café site is going to have separate pages, it can conceivably be one page broken into several sections. A simplified example, just using the headings for each section and no content, would look something like this:

```
<section>
      <h1>Introduction</h1>
</section>
<section>
      <h1>Recipes</h1>
</section>
<section>
      <h1>Menu</h1>
</section>
<section>
      <h1>Opening Times</h1>
</section>
<section>
      <h1>Contact</h1>
</section>
```

The <article> element

In the words of the specification, you can use an `<article>` element to mark-up "independent content." That's not the friendliest description, so it's useful to think of common examples such as a blog post, a forum post, a movie review, a news article, or an interactive widget.

The basic rule of thumb is that if the content can be syndicated or shared without the rest of the site context, it should be marked up as an article. For example, a short, glowing review of the Example Café might be marked up like the following example:

```
<article>
    <h1>Example Cafe, Great Food Delivered with
Superior Markup and Style</h1>
    <p>It's rare to find a restaurant that combines as
many exemplary elements as the example café. From the
superior markup of the café's website to the delicious
dishes served with care nothing about the Example Café
is left to chance.</p>
</article>
```

The <hr> element

The <hr> element creates a horizontal rule across the page. It is an empty element, rather like the <br> element.

```
<hr>
```

This is frequently used to separate distinct sections of a page where a new heading is not appropriate.

The <blockquote> element

When you want to quote a passage from another source, you should use the <blockquote> element. Note that there is a separate <q> element for use with smaller quotations, as discussed in the next section. Here's an example:

```
<p>The following description of the blockquote element
is taken from the WHATWG site:</p>
```

```
<blockquote> The blockquote element represents a
section that is quoted from another source. Content
inside a blockquote must be quoted from another source,
whose address, if it has one, may be cited in the cite
attribute.</blockquote>
```

Text inside a `<blockquote>` element is usually indented
from the left and right edges of the surrounding text, and
some browsers use an italicized font. (Use it only for quotes—
if you simply want an indented paragraph of text, use CSS.)

Using the cite attribute with the <blockquote> element

You can use the cite attribute on the `<blockquote>` element
to indicate the source of the quote. The value of this attribute
should be a URL pointing to an online document; if possible,
the exact place in that document. Browsers do not currently
do anything with this attribute, but it means the source of the
quote is there should you need it in the future.

```
<blockquote cite=
"http://developers.whatwg.org/grouping-
content.html#the-blockquote-element"> The blockquote
element represents a section that is quoted from
another source. Content inside a blockquote must be
quoted from another source, whose address, if it has
one, may be cited in the cite attribute.</blockquote>
```

The <aside> element

The `<aside>` element is used to mark-up related content
such as pull quotes, sidebars, and ads. The content in the aside
should be related to the surrounding content.

Pulling the first glowing sentence of the previous review illustrates a simple usage of the `<aside>` element.

```
<article>
    <h1>Example Cafe, Great Food Delivered with
Superior Markup and Style</h1>
    <p>It's rare to find a restaurant that combines as
many exemplary elements as the example café. From the
superior markup of the café's website to the delicious
dishes served with care nothing about the Example Café
is left to chance.</p>
    <aside> It's rare to find a restaurant that
combines as many exemplary elements as the example
café.</aside>
</article>
```

The <footer> element

Like the `<header>`, the `<footer>` was an extremely common class and id name found during Ian Hickson's survey of the web. A common usage of the footer is for legal copy. On some sites, such as those of pharmaceutical companies or financial services firms, this can be quite a large block of text, sometimes stretching to several screen's worth of text. Thankfully Example Café doesn't have quite the same legal and regulatory overhead, so you can just add a simple copyright notice into your `<footer>`.

```
<footer>  <p>All content copyright Example Café
2015</p>  </footer>
```

The <address> element

The <address> element is used to mark-up contact information for an article element or for the document as a whole. In this example you add it as contact information in the footer.

```
<footer>
    <address>For more information contact <a
href="mailto:examplecafe@example.com"> Example Café via
email</address>
    <p>All content copyright Example Café 2015</p>
</footer>
```

Lists

There are many reasons you might want to add a list to your pages, from putting your five favorite albums on your homepage to including a numbered set of instructions for visitors to follow (such as the steps you follow in the Try It Out examples in this book).
You can create three types of lists in HTML:

- Unordered: Like lists of bullet points
- Ordered: Use a sequence of numbers or letters instead of bullet points
- Definition: Enable you to specify a term and its definition

You can think of more uses for the lists as you meet them and start using them.

Using the <ul> element to Create unordered Lists

If you want to make a list of bullet points, write the list within the <ul> element (which stands for unordered list). Each bullet point or line you want to write should then be contained between opening <li> tags and closing </li> tags. (The li stands for list item.)

 You should always close the <li> element. Even though you might see some HTML pages that leave off the closing tag, this is a bad habit you should avoid. If you want to create a bulleted list, you can do so like this:

```
<ul>
     <li>Bullet point number one</li>
     <li>Bullet point number two</li>
     <li>Bullet point number three</li>
</ul>
```

You can check and see how this will look in a browser. As promised, the following shows the list of links from the illustration of the <nav> element reworked to use an unordered list. Navigation elements on the web are commonly marked up using lists, so it's useful to get used to that pattern as soon as possible.

```
<nav>
     <ul>
          <li><a href="recipes.html">Recipes</li>
          <li><a href="menu.html">Menu</a></li>
          <li><a href="opening_times.html">Opening
          Times</a></li>
          <li><a href-"contact.html">contact</a></li>
     </ul>
</nav>
```

The `<ul>` and `<li>` elements can carry all the universal attributes and UI event attributes.

Ordered Lists

Sometimes, you want your lists to be ordered. In an ordered list, rather than prefixing each point with a bullet point, you can use either numbers (1, 2, 3), letters (A, B, C), or Roman numerals (i, ii, iii) to prefix the list item.
An ordered list is contained inside the `<ol>` element. Each item in the list should then be nested inside the `<ol>` element and contained between opening `<li>` and closing `</li>` tags.

```
<ol>
      <li>Point number one</li>
      <li>Point number two</li>
      <li>Point number three</li>
</ol>
```

The results can be seen by opening the file in a browser.

Definition Lists

The HTML5 spec states `<dl>` are for description lists, which have a slightly wider remit than term and definition. "The `<dl>` element represents a description list, which consists of zero or more term-description (name/value) groupings; each grouping associates one or more terms/names (the contents of `<dt>` elements) with one or more descriptions/values (the contents of `<dd>` elements)."

The definition list is a special kind of list for providing terms followed by a short text definition or description for them. Definition lists are contained inside the <dl> element. The <dl> element then contains alternating <dt> and <dd> elements. The content of the <dt> element is the term you define. The <dd> element contains the definition of the previous <dt> element. For example, here is a definition list that describes the different types of lists in HTML:

```
<dl>
     <dt>Unordered List</dt>
     <dd>A list of bullet points.</dd>
     <dt>Ordered List</dt>
     <dd>An ordered list of points, such as a numbered
set of steps.</dd>
     <dt>Definition List</dt>
     <dd>A list of terms and definitions.</dd>
</dl>
```

Opening the file in a browser shows the results.

Nesting Lists

You can nest lists inside other lists. For example, you might want a numbered list with separate points corresponding to one of the list items. Number each nested list separately, unless you specify otherwise using the start attribute. And you should place each new list inside a <li> element.

```
<ol type="I">
     <li>Item one</li>
     <li>Item two</li>
     <li>Item three</li>
     <li>Item four
          <ol type="i">
               <li>Item 4.1</li>
```

```
            <li>Item 4.2</li>
            <li>Item 4.3</li>
        </ol>
    </li>
    <li>Item Five</li>
</ol>
```

Summary

In this chapter, you learned about the similarities between web pages and print documents; for example, a news story in print or on the web consists of a headline, some paragraphs of text, maybe some subheadings, and one or more pictures. On the web you need to explain the structure of these documents, and you can do that using HTML.

You know that HTML5 is the latest version of the HTML5 specification, and you know the special DOCTYPE used to put HTML documents into standards mode.

You have learned that the content of a web page is marked up using elements that describe the structure of the document. These elements consist of an opening tag, a closing tag, and some content between the opening and closing tags. To alter some properties of elements, the opening tag may carry attributes, and attributes are commonly written as name/value pairs. They can also be empty elements.

You also learned a lot of new elements and the attributes they can carry. You've seen how every HTML document should contain at least the `<html>`, `<head>`, `<title>`, and `<body>` elements. In the next chapter you learn about fine-tuning your text by adding meaning for humans and computers, more specific structure and other features that will greatly enrich your web pages.

Exercise

1. Mark up the following list with inserted and deleted content:

   Ricotta pancake ingredients:
   - 1 ½ ¾ cups ricotta;
   - ¾ cup milk;
   - 4 eggs;
   - 1 cup plain <u>white</u> flour;
   - 1 teaspoon baking powder;
   - ~~75g~~ <u>50g</u> butter;
   - Pinch of salt;

   - Answers at the end of the book.

Chapter 2: Text Structuring

Text Semantics

This section introduces a number of elements, which will help you more precisely describe text. Starting with elements that help you describe the importance or emphasis of text and working through elements that describe structured data such as time or represent programmatic code, this chapter adds a much richer set of tools to mark up your web pages.

The <span> element

The <span> element is a close cousin to the <div>. It's a generic element with no semantic value that you can use to group inline elements. So, if you have a part of a sentence or paragraph you want to group, you can use the <span> element. Here you can see a <span> element added to indicate which content refers to an inventor. It contains both a strong element and some text.

```
<div class="footnotes">
     <h2>Footnotes</h2>
     <p><span class="inventor"><strong>1</strong> The
World Wide Web was    invented by Tim Berners-
Lee</span></p>
     <p><strong>2</strong> The W3C is the World Wide
Web Consortium    which maintains many Web
standards</p>
</div>
```

On its own, this would have no effect on how the document looks visually, but it does add extra meaning to the markup, which now groups the related elements. It's particularly helpful to attach special styles to these elements using CSS rules.

The <em> element

The content of an <em> element is intended to be a point of emphasis in your document, and it usually displays in italicized text. The kind of emphasis intended is on words such as "must" in the following sentence:

```
<p>You <em>must</em> remember to close elements in
HTML.</p>
```

You should use this element only when you want to add emphasis to a word, not just because you want to make the text appear italicized. If you just want italic text for stylistic reasons — without adding emphasis — you can either use the <i> element or preferably use CSS.

The <strong> element

The <strong> element is intended to show strong emphasis for its content — stronger emphasis than the <em> element. As with the <em> element, you should use the <strong> element only when you want to add strong emphasis to part of a document. Most visual browsers display the strong emphasis in a bold font.

```
<p><em>Always</em> look at burning magnesium through
protective colored glass as it <strong>can cause
blindness</strong>.</p>
```

Open the file in a browser to see the results.

You need to remember that how the elements are presented (italics or bold) is largely irrelevant. You should use these elements to add emphasis to phrases and therefore give your documents greater meaning, rather than to control how they appear visually. It is quite simple with CSS to change the visual presentation of these elements—for example, to highlight any words inside an <em> element with a yellow background and make them bold rather than italic.

The <b> element

Anything that appears in a <b> element displays in bold, like the word "bold" here:

```
The following word uses a <b>bold</b> typeface.
```

For those interested in typography, it is worth noting that this does not necessarily mean the browser will use a boldface version of a font. Some browsers use an algorithm to take a normal version of a font and make the lines thicker (giving it the appearance of being bold).

The <i> element

The content of an <i> element displays in italicized text, like the word "italic" here:

```
The following word uses an <i>italic</i> typeface.
```

This does not necessarily mean the browser looks for an oblique or italicized version of the font. Most browsers use an algorithm to put the lines on a slant to simulate an italic font.

<strong> versus <b> and <em> versus <i>

You probably wonder why elements present the same way when shown in a browser and which one you should use. <strong> and <em> are generally recommended over <b> and <i> because the strength and emphasis aren't necessarily tied to typographic conventions. This means they can more sensibly be used in a screen reader or other implementation not dependent on a certain type style.

The <small> element

The <small> element is used for "fine print." Disclaimers, caveats, and copyrights are typical usages of the <small> element.

```
<small id="copyright">© Rob Larsen 2012</small>
```

The <cite> element

If you quote a text, you can indicate the source by placing it between an opening <cite> tag and a closing </cite> tag. As you would expect in a print publication, the content of the <cite> element renders in italicized text by default.

```
This chapter is taken from <cite>HTML
Programming</cite>.
```

If you reference an online resource, you should place your <cite> element inside an <a> element, which, as you see in Chapter 3, creates a link to the relevant document. There are several applications that potentially could make use of the <cite> element.

For example, a search application could use <cite> tags to find documents that reference certain works. Or a browser could collect the content of <cite> elements to generate a bibliography for any given document; although, at the moment it is not widely enough used for either feature to exist.

The <q> element

Use the <q> element when you want to add a quote within a sentence, rather than as an indented block on its own:

```
<p>As Dylan Thomas said, <q>Somebody's boring me. I
think it's me</q>.</p>
```

The HTML recommendation says that the text enclosed in a <q> element should begin and end in double quotes. Firefox inserts these quotation marks for you, but IE8 was the first version of Internet Explorer to support the <q> element. So, if you want your quote to be surrounded by quotation marks, be warned that IE7 and earlier versions of IE do not display them. If you still need to support IE7 and older, you can use CSS to fix this issue, so all is not lost. The <q> element can also carry the cite attribute. The value should be a URL pointing to the source of the quote.

The <dfn> element

The <dfn> element enables you to specify that you are introducing a special term.

Its use is similar to the italicized notes in this book used to introduce important new concepts. Typically, use the <dfn> element the first time you introduce a key term and only in that instance. Most recent browsers render the content of a <dfn> element in an italic font. For example, you can indicate that the term "HTML" in the following sentence is important and should be marked as such:

```
This book teaches you how to mark up your documents for
the Web using <dfn>HTML</dfn>.
```

Opening the file in a browser shows the results.

The <abbr> element

You can indicate when you use an abbreviated form or acronym by placing the abbreviation between opening <abbr> and closing </abbr> tags.
When possible, consider using a title attribute whose value is the full version of the abbreviations. For example, if you want to indicate that HTML is an acronym for HyperText Markup Language, you can use the <abbr> element like so:

```
This book teaches you how to mark up your documents for
the Web using <dfn> <abbr title="HyperText Markup
Language">HTML</abbr></dfn>
```

If you abbreviate a foreign word, you can also use the lang attribute to indicate the language used.

The \<time> element

You can use the \<time> element alongside the associated datetime attribute to markup text representing time in various forms. It consists of a \<time> element along with an optional datetime attribute. The contents of the \<time> element display in the browser, and the contents of the datetime attribute are designed to be a computer-readable representation of the same information. If you neglect to include a datetime attribute, the contents of the \<time> element must be in one of the formats supported by HTML.

Using a datetime attribute enables you to present a friendly date for your users and still leverage one of the more computer-useful representations. Marking up a valid date string with a more human-readable name might look like the following examples:

```
<time datetime="2013-1-1">New Year's Day 2013</time>
<time datetime="2004-10-27T20:25">On a late October
night</time>, the Boston Red Sox played in the decisive
game four of the 2004 World Series
The world marathon record now sits at <time
datetime="2h 3m 38s"> just over two hours</time>
```

The \<code> element

If your pages include any programming code (which is not uncommon on the web), the following four elements will be of particular use to you. You must place any code that you want to appear on a web page inside a \<code> element. Usually the content of the \<code> element is presented in a monospaced font, just like the code in most programming books (including this one).

WARNING When you are trying to display code on a web page (for example, if you were creating a page about web programming), and you want to include angled brackets, you cannot just use the opening and closing angle brackets inside these elements because the browser could mistake these characters for actual markup. Use < instead of the left-angle bracket (<), and use > instead of the right-angle bracket (>). These replacement sets of characters are known as escape codes or character entities.

Here is an example of the <code> element used to represent an <h1> element and its content in HTML:

```
<p><code>&lt;h1&gt;This is a primary
heading&lt;/h1&gt;</code></p>
```

Opening in a browser shows the results.
The <code> element is often used with the <pre> element so that the formatting of the code is retained.

<figure> and <figcaption> elements

You can use the <figure> element and the associated <figcaption> element to mark up and annotate figures or illustrations that might be referenced in text but aren't part of the main flow of the document. Using a small <code> element illustrates how you might use <figure> to illustrate some of the code from this book.

```
<figure id="14">
    <figcaption> using the code element to represent
an h1 element and its content in HTML</figcaption>
    <code>&lt;h1&gt;This is a primary
heading&lt;/h1&gt;</code> </figure>
```

The <var> element

The <var> element is another of the elements added to help programmers. You usually use it with the <pre> and <code> elements to indicate that the content of that element is a variable that can be supplied by a user.

```
<p><code>console.log( "<var>user-name</var>"
)</code></p>
```

Typically, the content of a <var> element is italicized.

The <samp> element

The <samp> element indicates sample output from a program, script, or the like. Again, it is mainly used when documenting programming concepts, for example:

```
<p>The following line uses the &lt;samp&gt; element to
indicate the output from a script or program.</p>
<p><samp>This is the output from our test
script.</samp></p>
```

This tends to display in a monospaced font, as you can see in a browser.

The <kbd> element

If, when talking about computers, you want to tell a reader to enter some text, you can use the <kbd> element to indicate what should be typed in, as in this example:

```
<p>To force quit an application in Windows, hold down
the <kbd>ctrl</kbd>, <kbd>alt</kbd> and
```

```
<kbd>delete</kbd> keys together.</p>
```

The content of a <kbd> element is usually represented in a monospaced font, rather like the content of the <code> element. Results can be seen in a browser.

The <sup> element

The content of a <sup> element is written in superscript; it displays one-half a character's height above the other characters and is also often slightly smaller than the text surrounding it.

```
Written on the 5<sup>th</sup> June.
```

The <sup> element is especially helpful to add exponential values to equations, and add the `st`, `nd`, `rd`, and `th` suffixes to numbers such as dates. However, in some browsers, you should be aware that it can create a taller gap between the line with the superscript text and the line above it.

The <sub> element

The content of a <sub> element is written in subscript; it displays one-half a character's height beneath the other characters and is also often slightly smaller than the text surrounding it.

```
The EPR paradox<sub>2</sub> was devised by Einstein,
Podolsky, and Rosen.
```

The <sub> element is particularly helpful to create footnotes.

The <mark> element

You can use the <mark> element to highlight text in a document. The goal of <mark> is to draw attention to content in a document outside of any emphasis the original author intended. Use this the same way you use a highlighter in a paper book, or as is common on some sites, use <mark> to indicate the presence of a particular search term in a block of text. The following code shows the word "HTML5" highlighted using <mark> in a block of text.

```
<p> This book focuses on the latest version of the
language, popularly referred to as <mark>HTML5</mark>.
There are two other versions you might encounter. These
are HTML 4.01, the last major versions of the language
from December 1999 and a stricter version from 2000
called XHTML (Extensible Hypertext Markup Language).
XHTML is still very popular in some applications so
important differences between it and <mark>HTML5</mark>
will be called out in the text. </p>
```

Editing Text

When working on a document with others, it helps if you can see changes that another person has made. Even when working on your own documents, it can be helpful to keep track of changes you make. Two elements are specifically designed for revising and editing text:

- The <ins> element for when you want to add text (usually shown underlined in a browser);
- The <del> element for when you want to delete some text (usually shown crossed out in a browser)

These features would also be particularly helpful as editing tools to note changes and modifications made by different authors.

NOTE If you are familiar with Microsoft Word, you'll see the <ins> and <del> elements are similar to a feature called Track Changes (which you can find under the Tools menu). The Track Changes feature underlines new text additions and crosses through deleted text.

NOTE You must be careful when using <ins> and <del> to ensure that you do not end up with a block-level element (such as a <p> or an <h2> element) inside an inline element (such as a <ins> or <del> element).

You can use the title attribute to provide information as to who added the <ins> or <del> element and why it was added or deleted. This information is offered to users as a tooltip in the major browsers.

You might also use the cite attribute on the <ins> and <del> element to indicate the source or reason for a change; although, this attribute is quite limiting because the value must be a URI.

The <ins> and <del> elements can also carry a datetime attribute whose value is a date and time in the following format:

```
YYYY-MM-DDThh:mm:ssTZD
```

This formula breaks down as follows:
- YYYY represents the year.
- MM represents the month.
- DD represents the day of the month.
- T is a separator between the date and time.
- hh is the hour.
- mm is the number of minutes.
- ss is the number of seconds.
- TZD is the time zone designator.

For example, `2013-04-16T20:30-05:00` represents 8:30 p.m. on April 16, 2013, according to U.S. Eastern Standard Time.

NOTE As you can see, the datetime attribute is rather long to be entered by hand and is more likely to be entered by a program that enables users to edit web pages.

Using Character entities for special characters

You can use most alphanumeric characters in your document, and they will display without a problem. However, some characters have special meaning in HTML, and for some characters you cannot enter a keyboard equivalent. For example, you cannot use the angle brackets that start and end tags because the browser can mistake them for markup. You can, however, use a set of different characters known as character entities to represent these special characters. Sometimes you also see character entities referred to as escape characters.

Comments

You can put comments between any tags in your HTML documents. Comments use the following syntax:

```
<!-- comment goes here -->
```

Anything after < ! -- until the closing --> does not display. It can still be seen in the source code for the document but is not shown onscreen.

It is good practice to comment your code, especially in complex documents, to indicate sections of a document and any other notes to anyone looking at the code.

You can even comment out whole sections of code. In the following snippet of code, you would not see the content of the <h2> element. You can also see comments indicating the section of the document, who added it, and when it was added.

```
<!-- Start of Footnotes Section added 04-24-04 by Bob
Stewart -->  <!-- <h2>Character Entities</h2> -->
<p><strong>Character entities</strong> can be used to
escape special  characters that the browser might
otherwise think have special meaning.</p> <!-- End of
Footnotes section -->
```

Summary

In this chapter, you learned a lot of new elements and the attributes they can carry to describe the structure of text:

- Presentational elements: <b>, <i>, <sup>, and <sub>
- Phrase elements: <em>, <strong>, <abbr>, <dfn>, <blockquote>, <q>, <cite>, <code>, <kbd>, <var>, and <samp>
- Editing elements: <ins> and <del>

You will obviously use some of these elements more than others, but where an element fits the content you want to mark up, from paragraphs to addresses, you should try to use these because structuring your text properly helps it last longer than if you just format it using line breaks. As browsers and search engines support more and more of these elements, you will gain additional benefit.

Exercises

1. Mark up the following sentence with the relevant presentational elements:

```
The 1st time the bold man wrote in italics, he
emphasized several key words.
```

2. You have already created the homepage for the Example Café site that you will build throughout the book. You also created a recipes page. Now you need to create three more pages so that you can continue to build the site in upcoming chapters. Each page should start like the homepage, with a level 1 heading titled example Café, followed by this paragraph: welcome to example Café. We will be developing this site throughout the book . After this:

   a. For a menu page, add a level 2 heading titled Menu. This should be followed by a paragraph saying, The menu will go here. Update the content of the <title> element to reflect that this page will feature the menus at the café. Save the file with the name menu.html.

   b. For an opening times page, add a level 2 heading saying opening hours. This should be followed by a paragraph saying, details of opening hours and how to find us will go here. Update the <title> element to reflect that the page tells visitors opening hours and where to find the café. Save the file with the name opening.html.

   c. For the contact page, add a level 2 heading titled Contact. This page should contain the address: 12 Sea View, newquay, Cornwall, uk. Update the <title> element to reflect that the page tells visitors how to contact the café.

- Answers at the end of the book.

Chapter 3: Links

Basic Links

You can specify a link using the <a> element. Anything between the opening <a> tag and the closing </a> tag becomes part of the link that users can click in a browser.

Linking to other Web Pages

To link to another web page, the opening <a> tag must carry an attribute called href; the value of the href attribute is the name of the file you are linking to.

For example, here is the <body> of a page. This page contains a link to a second page called index.html:

```
<body>
      <p>Return to the <a href="index.html">home
page</a>.</p>
</body>
```

As long as index.html is in the same folder as the first page, when you click the words "home page," the index.html page loads into the same window, replacing the current page.

URLS

A Uniform Resource Locator, or URL, specifies where you can find a resource on the web; you are probably most used to thinking of them as web addresses. As you move around the web, you see the URL of each web page in the address bar of your browser.

There are three key parts to the URL: the scheme, the host address, and the filepath.

The scheme identifies the way a file transmits. Most web pages use something called the HyperText Transfer Protocol (HTTP) to pass information to you, which is why most web pages start with http://. Although you might have noticed other prefixes such as https:// when doing banking online (which is a more secure form of http) or ftp:// when downloading large files.

The host address is usually the domain name for the site, for example, google.com. Often you see www before the domain name; although, it is not actually part of the domain name. The host address can also be a number called an IP address.

NOTE All computers connected to the Internet use an IP address. An IP address is a set of up to 12 digits separated by a period (full stop) symbol. When you enter a domain name into a browser, behind the scenes the name converts into the IP address for the computer(s) that stores the website. This is done by consulting a domain name server (DNS), which keeps a directory of domain names and the corresponding IP addresses. Interestingly, at one point, the Internet was running out of IP addresses, so the Internet Engineering Task Force (IETF) introduced Internet Protocol version 6 (IPv6), which is a new system of IP addressing that allows for many more available addresses.

Absolute and Relative URLs

An absolute URL contains everything you need to uniquely identify a particular file on the Internet. This is what you would type into the address bar of your browser to find a page. For example, to get the page about film on the fictional news site you met earlier in the chapter, you might type in the following URL.

```
http://www.exampleNewsSite.com/Entertainment/Film/index.html
```

As you can see, absolute URLs can quickly get quite long, and every page of a website can contain many links. When linking to a page on your own site, however, you can use a shorthand form: relative URLs.

A relative URL indicates where the resource is in relation to the current page. The examples earlier in this chapter, which link to another page in the same directory, are relative URLs. You can also use relative URLs to specify files in different directories. For example, imagine you are looking at the homepage for the entertainment section of the following fictional news site:

```
http://www.exampleNewsSite.com/Entertainment/index.html
```

You want to add a link to the index pages for each of the subsections: Film, TV, Arts, and Music. Rather than including the full URL for each page, you can use a relative URL, for example:

```
Film/index.html
TV/index.html
Arts/index.html
Music/index.html
```

Summary

In this chapter you learned about links. Links enable users to jump between pages and even between parts of an individual page (so that they don't have to scroll to find the place they need).

You have seen that you can use the <a> element to create source anchors, which are what most people think of when you mention links on the web. The content of the source anchor is what users can click— and this should usually be an informative, concise description of what users see when they click the link (rather than text such as "click here"), or it can be an image (as you see in Chapter 4, "Images, Audio, and Video").

You also learned how to link to specific parts of a page using the id attribute.

Along the way, you learned more about URLs, in particular the difference between an absolute URL, as with those that appear in the address bar of your browser, and relative URLs, which describe where a resource is in relation to the document containing it. Learning the different ways in which relative URLs can be used can also be helpful as you head to the next chapter and learn about adding images and other objects into your documents.

Chapter 4: Images, Video, Audio

Adding images

Images are added to a site using the <img> element, which must carry at least two attributes: the src attribute, indicating the source of the image, and an alt attribute, which provides a description of the image.

For example, the following line would add the image called logo.gif into the page (in this case, the image lives in a directory called images).

```
<img src="logo.gif" alt="Our logo" >
```

The src Attribute

The src attribute tells the browser where to find the image. The value is a URL and, just like the links you met in the previous chapter, the URL can be an absolute URL or a relative URL.

```
<img src="logo.gif" >
```

Generally speaking, images for your site should always reside on your server or on another server you control. It is not good practice to link to images on other sites because if the owner of the other site decides to move that image, your users will no longer see the image.

Because the images are on your server, rather than being an absolute URL, the value is more likely to be a relative URL that uses the same shorthand notations you met in the previous chapter when relative URLs were introduced.

Most web page authors create a separate directory (or folder) in the website for images. If you have a large site, you might even create different folders for different types of images. For example, you might keep any images used in the design of the interface (such as logos or buttons) separate from images used in the content of the site.

The alt Attribute

The alt attribute should appear on every <img> element and its value should be a text description of the image.

```
<img src="logo.gif" alt="Our logo" >
```

Often referred to as alt text, the value of this attribute should describe the image because of the following:

- If the browser cannot display the image, this text alternative is shown instead.

- Web users with visual impairments often use software called a screen reader to read a page to them, in which case the alt text describes the image they cannot see.

- Although search engines are clever, they cannot yet describe or index the contents of an image; therefore, providing a text alternative helps search engines index your pages and helps visitors find your site.

The height and width Attributes

The height and width attributes specify the height and width of the image, and the values for these attributes are almost always shown in pixels. (If you are not familiar with the concept of pixels, look at this in the section "Choosing the Right Image Format.")

```
<img src="logo.gif" alt="Wrox Logo" height="120"
width="180" >
```

Technically, the values of these attributes can be a percentage of the browser screen. Or if the image is inside an element that takes up only part of the page, known as a containing element, it would be a percentage of the containing element. If you do use a percentage, the number will be followed by a percent sign, but for most web pages this is rare, and showing an image at any size other than the size at which it was created can result in a distorted or fuzzy image.

Specifying the size of the image is considered good practice, so you should try to use these attributes on any image that you put on your pages.

It also helps a page to load faster and more smoothly because the browser knows how much space to allocate to the image, and it can correctly render the rest of the page while the image is still loading.

Video and Audio

Adding YouTube Movies to Web Pages

By far, the most common way to host and share video is with Google's YouTube service. Whether you upload your own content or want to share content from another YouTube user, the method to embed the video is the same.

YouTube has made it easy for users to embed the YouTube Player on their pages. This is done simply by copying and pasting a line of code from the YouTube site into any web page.

Looking at it you see that it introduces a new element, the <iframe>. The <iframe> element doesn't, by itself, have anything to do with video. The <iframe>, or inline frame, is a special element that enables you to embed another web page within a web page using the familiar src attribute. By embedding the <iframe> from YouTube in a small corner of your site, you can always be sure to get the latest content and code that YouTube offers. All it takes is to paste that small <iframe> code snippet anywhere within the body of your page, and you have a world-class video solution.

Adding rich Media with the <audio> and <video> elements

Any rich media solution for the modern web starts with the new <audio> and <video> elements, which work similarly, so many of the lessons you learn about one applies to the other. You focus mostly on <video> in this section, but you see an example of <audio> in action as well.

<video> is designed to work just like the <img> element you learned about earlier in this chapter. The most basic usage is a <video> element with src, height, and width attributes. As a note, this and the following examples in this section work only in Internet Explorer 9, Chrome, and Safari. You learn why that is in the upcoming section on containers and codecs.

```
<video width="720" height="480" src="central.mp4">
```

In addition to the global attributes, <video> supports the following attributes:

```
poster preload autoplay mediagroup loop muted controls
crossorigin
```

Adding Audio to Web Pages with the <audio> Element

As you learned, the <audio> element works the same way as the <video> element. As the following code sample shows, an <audio> element and an src attribute are enough to get audio onto your pages.

```
<audio src="audio/pink_noise.mp3">
```

<audio> also supports the following attributes that you learned about earlier in the chapter:

```
crossorigin preload autoplay loop muted controls
```

Summary

In this chapter, you learned how to make your pages look more exciting by adding images and other multimedia objects. Images can add life to a page, but they can also increase the time it takes to load a page. Therefore, it pays to save any images you want to show on the web in JPEG, GIF, or PNG formats, which compress well (creating smaller files) while retaining quality.

Then, you saw how to add video and audio to your site. You learned that the easiest way to do this is to leverage a third-party service such as YouTube.

Now you should be well equipped to add images and rich media to your pages to make them look appealing and attract more visitors.

Exercises

1. Add images (use any image you find suitable) of icons representing a diary, a camera and a newspaper to the following example:

```
<h1>Icons</h1>
<p>Here is an icon used to represent a diary.</p>
<img src="images/diary.gif" alt="Diary" width="150"
height="120" >

<p>Here is an icon used to represent a picture.</p>
Camera image goes here

<p>Here is an icon used to represent a news item.</p>

Newspaper image goes here
```

   - Answers at the end of the book.

Chapter 5: Tables

To work with tables, you need to start thinking in grids, so start by looking at some examples of how popular websites use tables.

You create a table in HTML using the <table> element. Inside the <table> element, the table is written out row by row. A row is contained inside a <tr> element, which stands for table row. Each cell is then written inside the row element using a <td> element, which stands for table data. Following is the code used to create this basic table:

```
<table border="1">
     <tr>
          <td>Row 1, Column 1</td>
          <td>Row 1, Column 2</td>
     </tr>
     <tr>
          <td>Row 2, Column 1</td>
          <td>Row 2, Column 2</td>
     </tr>
</table>
```

When writing code for a table in a text editor, you should start each row and cell on a new line and indent table cells inside table rows as shown. If you use a web page authoring tool such as Dreamweaver, it probably automatically indents the code for you.

Many web page authors find it particularly helpful to indent the code for a table because leaving off just one tag in a table can prevent the entire table from displaying properly. Indenting the code makes it easier to keep track of the opening and closing of each element. Take a look at the same code again. This time, it has not been split onto separate lines or indented, which is much harder to read.

```
<table border="1"><tr><td>Row 1, Column 1</td><td>Row
1, Column 2</td></tr><tr> <td>Row 2, Column
```

```
1</td><td>Row 2, Column 2</td></tr></table>
```

All tables follow this basic structure; although additional elements and attributes enable you to control the presentation of tables. If a row or column should contain a heading, use a <th> element in place of the <td> element for the cells that contain a heading. By default, most browsers render the content of a <th> element in bold text.

WARNING *Each cell must be represented by either a <td> or a <th> element for the table to display correctly, even if there is no data in that cell.*

Now take a look at a slightly more complicated table. This time the table includes headings. In this example, the table shows a financial summary for a small company.

Here is the code used to create this table:

```
<table border="1">
    <tr>
        <th></th>
        <th>Outgoings ($)</th>
        <th>Receipts ($)</th>
        <th>Profit ($)</th>
    </tr>
    <tr>
        <th>Quarter 1 (Jan-Mar)</th>
        <td>11200.00</td>
        <td>21800.00</td>
        <td><b>10600.00</b></td>
    </tr>
        <tr>
        <th>Quarter 2 (Apr-Jun)</th>
        <td>11700.00</td>
        <td>22500.00</td>
        <td><b>10800.00</b></td>
    </tr>
```

```
        <tr>
                <th>Quarter 3 (Jul - Sep)</th>
                <td>11650.00</td>
                <td>22100.00</td>
                <td><b>10450.00</b></td>
        </tr>
        <tr>
                <th>Quarter 4 (Oct - Dec)</th>
                <td>11850.00</td>
                <td>22900.00</td>
                <td><b>11050.00</b></td>
        </tr>
</table>
```

The first row is made entirely of headings for outgoings, receipts, and profit. The top-left cell is empty; in the code for the table; you still need an empty <td> element to tell the browser that this cell is empty. (Otherwise it has no way to know that there is an empty cell.)

In each row, the first cell is also a table heading cell (indicated using a <th>), which states which quarter the results are for. Then the remaining three cells of each row contain table data contained inside the <td> elements.

The figures showing the profit (in the right column) are contained within a <b> element, which shows the profit figures in a bold typeface. This demonstrates how any cell can contain all manner of markup. The only constraint on placing markup inside a table is that it must nest within the table cell element (whether a <td> or a <th> element). You cannot have an opening tag for an element inside a table cell and a closing tag outside that cell—or vice versa.

When creating tables, many people do not actually bother with the <th> element and instead use the <td> element for every cell—including headers. You should, however, aim to use the <th> element whenever you have a table heading. This is especially true when you use the scope attribute (which you learn about in the next section, "Basic Table Elements and Attributes"), as it is valid only for <th> elements.

NOTE As you can see from the examples so far in this chapter, tables can take up a lot of space and make a document longer, but clear formatting of tables makes it much easier to see what is going on in your code. No matter how familiar the code looks when you write it, you will be glad that you made good use of structure if you have to come back to it a year later. Most good code editors have the option to format HTML automatically. No matter what code editor you use, you should familiarize yourself with the tools available to automatically format code for you.

Basic Table Elements and Attributes

Now that you've seen how basic tables work, this section describes the elements in a little more detail, introducing the attributes they can carry. Some of the attributes enable you to create more sophisticated table layouts. Skim through this section quickly; when you know what you can do with the markup, you can always come back again and study the markup closely to see how to achieve what you want.

The <table> element

Creates a Table The <table> element is the containing element for all tables. It can carry the following attributes:

- All the universal attributes
- Basic event attributes for scripting

The dir Attribute

The dir attribute is supposed to indicate the direction of text used in the table. Possible values are ltr for left to right text and rtl for right to left (for languages such as Hebrew and Arabic):

```
dir="rtl"
```

If you use the dir attribute with a value of rtl on the <table> element, the cells appear from the right first, and each consecutive cell is placed to the left of that one.

The <tr> element Contains Table Rows

The <tr> element contains each row in a table. Anything appearing within a <tr> element should appear on the same row.

The <td> and <th> elements Represent Table Cells

Every cell in a table is represented by either a <td> element for cells containing table data or a <th> element for cells containing table headings.

By default, the contents of a <th> element usually display in a bold font, horizontally aligned in the center of the cell. The content of a <td> element, meanwhile, usually displays left-aligned and not in bold (unless otherwise indicated by CSS or another element).

The <td> and <th> elements can both carry the same set of attributes, and the attribute applies only to that one cell carrying it. Any effects these attributes have override settings for the table as a whole or any containing element (such as a row).

In addition to the universal attributes and the basic event attributes, the <td> and <th> elements can also carry the following attributes:

```
colspan headers rowspan
```

<th> elements can also carry the scope attribute.

The colspan Attribute

Use the colspan attribute when a cell should span across more than one column. The value of the attribute specifies how many columns of the table a cell spans across. (See the section "Spanning Columns Using the colspan Attribute.")

```
colspan="2"
```

The headers Attribute

The headers attribute indicates which headers correspond to that cell. The value of the attribute is a space-separated list of the header cells' id attribute values:

```
headers="income q1"
```

The main purpose of this attribute is to support voice browsers. When a table is read to you, it can be hard to keep track of which row and column you are on; therefore, the header attribute reminds users which row and column the current cell's data belongs to.

The rowspan Attribute

The rowspan attribute specifies the number of rows of the table a cell spans across, the value of the attribute being the number of rows the cell stretches across. (See the example in the section "Spanning Rows Using the rowspan Attribute.")

```
rowspan="2"
```

The scope Attribute

You can use the scope attribute to indicate which cells the current header provides a label or header information for. You can use it instead of the headers attribute in basic tables, but it does not have much support.

```
scope="range"
```

Adding a Caption to a Table

Whether your table shows results for a scientific experiment, values of stocks in a particular market, or what is on television tonight, each table should have a caption so that visitors to your site know what the table is for.

Even if the surrounding text describes the content of the table, it is good practice to give the table a formal caption using the <caption> element. By default, most browsers display the contents of this element centred above the table, as shown in the next section.

The <caption> element appears directly after the opening <table> tag; it should come before the first row:

```
<table>
      <caption> Opening hours for the Example
Cafe</caption>
            <tr>
```

By using a <caption> element, rather than just describing the purpose of the table in a previous or subsequent paragraph, you are directly associating the content of the table with this description—and this association can be used by screen readers and by applications that process web pages (such as search engines).

Grouping Sections of a Table

In this section, you look at some techniques that enable you to group together cells, rows, and columns of a table, and learn the advantages that doing this can bring. In particular, you see how to do the following:

- Use the rowspan and colspan attributes to make cells stretch over more than one row or column.

- Split a table into three sections: a head, body, and foot.

- Group columns using the <colgroup> element.

- Share attributes between unrelated columns using the <col> element.

Spanning Columns using the colspan attribute

As you saw when looking at the <td> and <th> elements, both can carry an attribute called colspan that enables the table cell to span (or stretch) across more than one column.

The next example shows a table that has three rows; the cells of the table are shaded to illustrate the colspan attribute in action:

- The first row has three columns of equal width, and there is one cell for each column.

- In the second row, the first cell is the width of one column, but the second cell spans the width of two columns.

- The third row has just one cell that spans all three columns.

Here is the code:

```
<table>
<caption>Spanning columns using the colspan
```

```
attribute</caption>
      <tr>
            <td class="one"> </td>
            <td class="two"> </td>
            <td class="three"> </td>
      </tr>
      <tr>
            <td class="one"> </td>
            <td colspan="2" class="two"> </td>
      </tr>
      <tr>
            <td colspan="3" class="one"> </td>
      </tr>
</table>
```

In the first row, you can see that there are three <td> elements, one for each cell.

In the second row, there are only two <td> elements, and the second of these elements carries a colspan attribute. The value of the colspan attribute indicates how many columns the cell should stretch across. In this case, the second cell spans two columns; therefore, it has a value of 2.

In the final row, there is just one <td> element, and this time the colspan attribute has a value of 3, which indicates that it should take up three columns.

As mentioned at the start of this chapter, when dealing with tables you must think in terms of grids. This grid is three cells wide and three rows tall, so the middle row could not have two equal-sized cells. (Because they would not fit in the grid—you cannot have a cell spanning 1.5 columns.)

An example of where the colspan attribute might be useful is in creating a timetable or schedule where the day is divided into hours—some slots lasting 1 hour, others lasting 2 to 3 hours.

You might also have noticed the use of the nonbreaking space character ( ) in the cells, which is included so that the cell has some content; without content for a table cell, some browsers cannot display the background color.

Spanning rows using the rowspan attribute

The rowspan attribute does much the same thing as the colspan attribute, but it works in the opposite direction: It enables cells to stretch vertically across cells. You can see the effect of the rowspan attribute in the next example. When you use a rowspan attribute, the corresponding cell in the row beneath it must be left out:

```
<table>
<caption>Spanning rows using the rowspan
attribute</caption>
    <tr>
        <td class="one"> </td>
        <td class="two"> </td>
        <td rowspan="3" class="three"> </td>
    </tr>
    <tr>
        <td class="one"> </td>
        <td rowspan="2" class="two"> </td>
    </tr>
    <tr>
        <td class="one"> </td>
    </tr>
</table>
```

Splitting up Tables using a Head, Body, and Foot

There are occasions in which you may want to distinguish between the body of a table (where most of the data is held) and the headings or maybe even the footers. For example, think of a bank statement: You may have a table where the header contains column headings, the body contains a list of transactions, and the footer contains the balance in the account.

If the table is too long to show on a screen, the header and footer might remain in view all the time, whereas the body of the table gains a scrollbar. Similarly, when printing a long table that spreads over more than one page, you might want the browser to print the head and foot of a table on each page. Unfortunately, the main browsers do not yet support these ideas, although there are options to implement this using CSS or JavaScript. However, if you add these elements to your tables, you can use CSS to attach different styles to the contents of the <thead>, <tbody>, and <tfoot> elements. It can also help those who use aural browsers, which read pages to users.

The three elements for separating the head, body, and foot of a table follow:

- <thead> to create a separate table header
- <tbody> to indicate the main body of the table
- <tfoot> to create a separate table footer

A table may also contain several <tbody> elements to indicate different "pages," or groups of data.

Consider the following example:

```
<table>
     <thead>
          <tr>
               <th>Transaction date</th>
               <th>Payment type and details</th>
               <th>Paid out</th>
               <th>Paid in</th>
               <th>Balance</th>
          </tr>
     </thead>
     <tfoot>
          <tr>
               <td></td>
               <td></td>
               <td>$1970.27</td>
               <td>$2450.00</td>
```

```html
            <td>$8940.88</td>
        </tr>
</tfoot>
<tbody>
        <tr>
            <td>12 Jun 12</td>
            <td>Amazon.com</td>
            <td>$49.99</td>
            <td></td>
            <td>$8411.16</td>
        </tr>
        <tr>
            <td>13 Jun 12</td>
            <td>Total</td>
            <td>$60.00</td>
            <td></td>
            <td>$8351.16</td>
        </tr>
        <tr>
            <td>14 Jun 12</td>
            <td>Whole Foods</td>
            <td>$75.28</td>
            <td></td>
            <td>$8275.88</td>
        </tr>
        <tr>
            <td>14 Jun 12</td>
            <td>Visa Payment</td>
            <td>$350.00</td>
            <td></td>
            <td>$7925.88</td>
        </tr>
        <tr>
            <td>15 Jun 12</td>
            <td>Cheque 122501</td>
            <td></td>
            <td>$1450.00</td>
            <td>$9375.88</td>
        </tr>
</tbody>
<tbody>
```

```
        <tr>
                <td>17 Jun 12</td>
                <td>Murco</td>
                <td>$60.00</td>
                <td></td>
                <td>$9315.88</td>
        </tr>
        <tr>
                <td>18 Jun 12</td>
                <td> </td>
                <td></td>
                <td>$1000.00</td>
                <td>$10315.88</td>
        </tr>
        <tr>
                <td>18 Jun 12</td>
                <td>McLellans Bakery</td>
                <td>$25.00</td>
                <td></td>
                <td>$10290.88</td>
        </tr>
        <tr>
                <td>18 Jun 12</td>
                <td>Apple Store</td>
                <td>$1350.00</td>
                <td></td>
                <td>$8940.88</td>
        </tr>
    </tbody>
</table>
```

Summary

In this chapter, you have seen how tables can be a powerful tool when creating pages. You have seen how all tables are based on a grid pattern and use the four basic elements: <table>, which contains each table; <tr>, which contains the rows of a table; <td>, which contains a cell of table data; and <th>, which represents a cell that contains a heading.

You have also seen how you can add headers, footers, and captions to tables. It is particularly helpful to add a <thead> and <tfoot> element to any table that may be longer than a browser window or sheet of printed paper because these could help a reader relate between the content and the information in headers or footers.

You can now make cells span both columns and rows; although, you should avoid doing this in tables that contain data because it makes them harder for aural browsers to read to a user. You have also seen how to group columns so that you can preserve structure, and so they can share styles and attributes.

Finally, you saw some of the accessibility issues for the use of tables. You must be aware of the process of linearization, which a screen reader performs before reading a table to a user, so that your sites are accessible to users with visual impairments. You also need to know how to provide extra information that indicates the headers for each cell.

In the next chapter, you learn about using forms to collect information from visitors.

Exercises

1. Where should the `<caption>` element for a table be placed in the document and, by default, where is it displayed?

- Answers at the end of the book.

Chapter 6: Forms

Any form that you create lives inside a <form> element, and the form controls (the text input boxes, drop-down boxes, check boxes, a submit button, and so on) live between the opening <form> and closing </form> tags. A <form> element can also contain other HTML markup as you would find in the rest of a page.

After users enter information into a form, they usually must click a submit button. (Although the actual text on the button may say something different such as Search, Send, or Proceed — and often pressing the Return key on the keyboard has the same effect as clicking this button.) This indicates that the user has filled out the form, and this usually sends the form data to a web server.

On a traditional web page, after form data arrives at the server, a script or other program processes the data and sends a new web page back to you. The returned page responds to a request you have made or acknowledges an action you have taken. There's a variation on this called Ajax that you'll learn at some other point in your learning where all these actions take place on the same page. The rest of this chapter focuses on the traditional pattern.

For example, you might want to add the search form shown to your page. You can see that this form contains a textbox for users to enter the keywords of what they are searching for, and a submit button with the word Search on it. When users click the Search button, the information is sent to the server, which then processes the data and generates a new page for users telling what pages meet the search criteria.

When a browser sends data to the server, it is transmitted in name/value pairs. The name corresponds to the name of the form control, and the value is what the user has entered (if the user can type an answer) or the value of the option selected (if there is a list of options to choose from).

Each item needs both a name and a value because if you have five textboxes on a form, you need to know which data corresponds to which textbox. The processing application can then process the information from each form control individually.

The <form> element carries an attribute called action whose value is the URL of the page on the web server that handles search requests. Meanwhile, the method attribute indicates which of two HTTP methods—get and post—are used in getting the form data to the server.

To create forms, you first need to look at the <form> element in a little more detail and then go through the different types of form controls to see how they sit inside the <form> element.

Creating a Form with The <form> element

As you have already seen, forms live inside an element called <form>. The <form> element can also contain other markup, such as paragraphs, headings, and so on; although, it may not contain another <form> element.

Providing you keep your <form> elements separate from each other (and no <form> element contains another <form> element), your page may contain as many forms as you like. For example, you might have a login form, a search form, and a form to subscribe to a newsletter, all on the same page. If you do have more than one form on a page, users can send the data from only one form at a time to the server.

In a traditional web page, every <form> element should carry at least two attributes:

```
action method
```

A <form> element may also carry all the universal attributes and the following attributes:

```
enctype novalidate target autocomplete accept-charset
```

The action attribute

The action attribute indicates what happens to the data when the form is submitted. Usually, the value of the action attribute is a page or program on a web server that receives the information.
For example, if you have a login form consisting of a username and password, the details the user enters may get passed to a page written in ASP.NET on the web server called login.aspx, in which case the action attribute could read as follows:

```
<form
action="http://www.example.org/membership/login.aspx">
```

The method attribute

Form data can be sent to the server in two ways, each corresponding to an HTTP method:
- The get method, which sends data as part of the URL. This is the default.
- The post method, which hides data in the HTTP headers.

You learn more about these two methods in the section "Sending Form Data to the Server," where you learn what they mean and when you should use each one.

The id attribute

The id attribute enables you to uniquely identify the <form> element within a page, just as you can use it to uniquely identify any element on a page.

It is good practice to give every <form> element an id attribute because many forms make use of style sheets and scripts, which may require the use of the id attribute to identify the form.

The value of the id attribute should be unique within the document and should also follow the other rules for values of the id attribute mentioned in Chapter 1, "Structuring Documents for the Web." Some people start the value of id and name attributes for forms with the characters frm and then use the rest of the value to describe the kind of data the form collects—for example, frmLogin or frmSearch.

The name attribute

As you have already seen through its use on other elements, the name attribute is the predecessor to the id attribute, and as with the id attribute, the value should be unique to the document.

Generally, you do not need to use this attribute, but when you do use it, you can give it the same value as the id attribute. You often see the value of this attribute begin with the characters frm followed by the purpose of the form (such as frmLogin or frmSearch).

The enctype attribute

If you use the HTTP post method to send data to the server, you can use the enctype attribute to specify how the browser encodes the data before it sends it to the server. Browsers tend to support three types of encoding:

- `application/x-www-form-urlencoded`, which is the standard method most forms use. Browsers use this because some characters, such as spaces, the plus sign, and some other nonalphanumeric characters, cannot be sent to the web server. Instead, they are replaced by other characters that are used to represent them.
- `multipart/form-data`, which enables the data to be sent in parts, where each consecutive part corresponds to a form control, in the order it appears in the form. It is commonly used when visitors need to upload files (such as photos) to a server. Each part can have an optional content-type header of its own indicating the type of data for that form control.
- `text/plain`, which sends the data to the server as unmodified, plain text.

If this attribute is not used, browsers use the first value. As a result, you are likely to use this attribute only if your form allows users to upload a file (such as an image) to the server, or if they are going to use non-ASCII characters, in which case the enctype attribute should be given the second value:

```
enctype="multipart/form-data"
```

The accept-charset attribute

Different languages are written in different character sets or groups of characters. However, when creating websites, developers do not always build them to understand all different languages.

The idea behind the accept-charset attribute is that it specifies a list of character encodings that a user may enter and that the server can then process. Values should be a space-separated or comma-delimited list of character sets. For example, the following indicates that a server accepts UTF-8 encodings:

```
accept-charset="utf-8"
```

If no accept-charset attribute is set, any character set is valid.

The novalidate attribute

The novalidate attribute is a boolean attribute that indicates whether the form should be validated when submitted. If present, the browser should not validate the form prior to submission.

```
<form
action="http://www.example.org/membership/login.aspx"
novalidate >
```

This attribute is currently supported in Chrome 6+, Firefox 4+, Opera 10.6+, and Internet Explorer 10+.

The target attribute

The target attribute specifies a named window or keyword for the processing of the form submission. To process a form in a new window, for example, you could set the target of a <form> element to "_blank".

```
<form
action="http://www.example.org/membership/login.aspx"
target="_blank" >
```

The autocomplete attribute

This attribute indicates whether or not the browser should auto-fill form values. Setting it to off indicates that the browser should not auto-fill any values. The default value is on.

```
<form
action="http://www.example.org/membership/login.aspx"
autocomplete="off" >
```

This attribute is currently supported in Chrome 17+, Firefox 4+, Safari 5.2+, and Opera 10.6+.

Form Controls

This section covers the different types of form controls that live inside the <form> element to collect data from a visitor to your site, including:

- Text input controls, including many new HTML5 inputs
- Buttons
- Check boxes and radio buttons
- Select boxes (sometimes referred to as drop-down menus and list boxes)
- File select boxes
- New HTML5 form elements such as progress bars and meters
- Hidden controls

Text Inputs

Text input boxes are used on many web pages. Possibly the most famous text input box is the one in the middle of the Google homepage that enables you to enter what you want to search for.

On a printed form, the equivalent of a text input is a box or line on which you write a response.

For a long time there were only three types of text input used on forms:

- **Single-line text input controls**: Used for items that require only one line of user input. They are created using the <input> element and sometimes referred to simply as textboxes.
- **Password input controls:** These are just like the single-line text input, except they mask the characters a user enters so that the characters cannot be seen on the screen. They tend to show either an asterisk or a dot instead of each character the user types so that someone cannot simply look at the screen to see what a user types in. Password input controls are mainly used for entering passwords on login forms or sensitive details such as credit card numbers. They are also created using the <input> element.
- **Multiline text input controls**: Used when the user is required to give details that may be longer than a single sentence. Multiline input controls are created with the <textarea> element.

This simple view has changed with HTML5. The HTML5 specification added many new types of <input> elements that correspond to common types of data on the web. The list of new <input> elements follows:

- **color**: For choosing a color by using a color wheel.
- **date**: For entering a calendar date.
- **datetime**: For entering a date and time with the time zone set to Greenwich/Universal Time.
- **datetime-local**: For entering a local date and time.
- **email**: For entering either a single e-mail address or a list of e-mail addresses. Multiple addresses can be entered in a comma-separated list.
- **month**: For entering a year and month.
- **number**: For numerical input.
- **range**: Unlike the normal text inputs in this list, this input type is generally represented as a slider that enables the user to choose a value from a range of numerical values.

- **search**: For entering search terms.
- **tel**: For entering telephone numbers.
- **time**: For entering a time consisting of hours, minutes, seconds, and fractional seconds.
- **url**: For entering website URLs.
- **week**: For entering a date that is made up of a year and week number. An example of this format is 2013-W01 for the first week of 2013.

Single-Line Text Input Controls

The most basic single-line text input controls are created using an <input> element whose type attribute has a value of text. Here is a basic example of a single-line text input used for a search box:

```
<form action="http://www.example.org/search.aspx"
method="get" name="frmSearch">
    <p>Search:<br>
    <input type="text" name="txtSearch" value="Search
for" size="20" maxlength="64"></p>
    <p><input type="submit" value="Submit"></p>
</form>
```

Open the file in a browser to see the results.

NOTE *Just as some people try to start form names with the characters frm, it is also common to start text input names with the characters txt to indicate that the form control is a textbox. This can be particularly handy when working with the data on the server to remind you what sort of form control sent that data. However, some programmers prefer not to use this notation, so if you work with someone else on a project, it is worth discussing that person's preference at the start of the work.*

Attribute	Purpose
name	This attribute is also required and gives the name part of the name/value pair sent to the server . (Remember: Each control on a form is represented as a name/ value pair where the name identifies the form control, and the value is what the user entered .)
value	Provides an initial value for the text input control that the user sees when the form loads . You would use this attribute only if you want something to be written in the text input when the page loads (such as a cue to tell users what they should enter) . The new placeholder attribute does a better job at this hinting task . The value attribute is also used for scripting.
size	Enables you to specify the width of the text input control in terms of characters; the search box in the earlier example is 20 characters wide . The size property does not affect how many characters users can enter (in this case they could enter 40 characters even when the size property has a value of 20); it just indicates how many characters

	wide the input will be . If users enter more characters than the size of the input, they can scroll right and left using the arrow keys to see what they have entered .
`maxlength`	Enables you to specify the maximum number of characters a user can enter into the textbox . Usually after the maximum number of characters has been entered, even if the user keeps pressing more keys, no new characters will be added .
`placeholder`	Represents a short hint that displays as the initial value in the input field .

Password Input Controls

If you want to collect sensitive data such as passwords and credit card information, you can use the password input. The password input masks the characters the user types on the screen by replacing them with either a dot or an asterisk, so that they would not be visible to someone looking over the user's shoulder.

Password input controls are created almost identically to the single-line text input controls, except that the type attribute on the <input> element is given a value of password.

Here you can see an example of a login form that combines a single-line text input control and a password input control:

```
<form action="http://www.example.com/login.asp"
method="post">
      <p>Username:<br>
      <input type="text" name="txtUsername" value=""
size="20" maxlength="20"></p>
      <p>Password:
      <input type="password" name="pwdPassword"
value="" size="20" maxlength="20"></p>
      <p><input type="submit" value="Log in"></p>
</form>
```

NOTE As you can see, it is common to start the name of any password with the characters pwd so that when you come to deal with the data on the server, you know the associated value came from a password input box.

NOTE Although passwords are hidden on the screen, they are still sent across the Internet as clear text, which is not considered secure. To make them secure you must use an SSL connection between the client and server and encrypt any sensitive data (such as passwords and credit card details). SSL connections and encryption should be covered in a book about server-side languages such as ASP.NET and PHP.

Multiple-Line Text Input Controls

If you want to allow a visitor to your site to enter more than one line of text, you must create a multiple-line text input control using the <textarea> element.
Here is an example of a multiple-line text input used to collect feedback from visitors to a site:

```
<form action="http://www.example.org/feedback.asp"
method="post">
      <p>Please tell us what you think of the site and
      then click submit:</p>
```

```
<textarea name="txtFeedback" rows="20" cols="50">
Enter your feedback here.
</textarea>
<p><input type="submit" value="Submit"></p>
</form>
```

The text inside the <textarea> element is not indented (in the same way that other code in this book is indented). Anything written between the opening and closing <textarea> tags is treated as if it were written inside a <pre> element, and formatting of the source document is preserved. If the words "Enter your feedback here" were indented in the code, they would also be indented in the resulting multiline text input on the browser.

Attribute	Purpose
name	The name of the control. This is used in the name/value pair that is sent to the server
rows	Used to specify the size of a <textarea>; it indicates the number of rows of text a <textarea> element should have and therefore corresponds to the height of the text area.
cols	Used to specify the size of a <textarea>; it specifies the number of columns of text and therefore corresponds to the width of the box. One column is the average width of a character.
maxlength	Maximum number of characters the user can enter.

autofocus	Boolean attribute that indicates that the element should have focus when the page loads.
required	Boolean attribute that indicates whether the input is a required element.
placeholder	Specifies a sample value to show users as a hint.
dirname	Provides a name for a text directional hint.
wrap	Specifies whether the text in a text area should be forced to wrap at the value of the cols attribute.
disabled	Boolean attribute that disables the select box, preventing user intervention.
form	Indicates the association <form> element for the <textarea> element. Value represents the id of the associated <form>.
readonly	Boolean attribute that indicates whether the user can edit the form field.

The <textarea> element can also take all the universal attributes.

By default, when a user runs out of columns in a <textarea>, the text is wrapped onto the next line (which means it just flows onto the next line as text in a word processor does), but the server receives it as if it were all on one line. Because some users expect the sentences to break where they see them break on the screen, the wrap attribute enables you to indicate how the text should be wrapped. Possible values are as follows:

- `soft` (the default), which means wherever the text wraps, users see it on the new line, but it is transmitted to the server as if it were all on the same line, unless users press the Enter key, in which case it is treated as a line break.
- `hard`, which means wherever the text wraps, it is transmitted to the server as a new line.

Using placeholders to Illustrate Example Input

As you saw in the section on basic inputs, the value attribute is often used to provide a sample input. The downside to this technique is that users don't always clear the input so that example text is often included as part of the data sent to the server. To fix this, people script the input to show a default value until the input is given focus. Focus indicates that the form element is the current one being interacted with by the user.

After a form element has focus, the JavaScript can clear out the input value and ready the form field for user input. The placeholder attribute replicates this behavior without the need for scripting.

Ensuring User Privacy and Security with the autocomplete Attribute

Web browsers typically offer the ability to save form entries to save time when filling out forms with similar information. This is a convenient feature, but there are times where this is dangerous behavior. For example, saving and redisplaying a credit card number, bank account number, or Social Security code could be catastrophic if you entered that information on a public computer. Similarly, login and password information can be convenient to have prepopulated, but it's a serious security hole.

Setting the autocomplete attribute allows web authors to control whether form entries should be cached. `autocomplete` takes two different values: on and off. on indicates that the values are safe to save and prepopulate. off indicates that they should not be saved.

Ensuring information is provided with the required Attribute

Often information in a form is required. For example, if you request an insurance quote for your car, the make and model of the car and the address where it's parked at night would be information needed to provide a reasonable quote.

In those cases you can use the required attribute to ensure that the form will be submitted only if there's content in the required fields.

Buttons

Buttons are most commonly used to submit a form; although, they are sometimes used to clear or reset a form and even to trigger client-side scripts. (For example, on a basic loan calculator form within the page, a button might be used to trigger the script that calculates repayments without sending the data to the server.) You can create a button in three ways:

- Using an <input> element with a type attribute whose value is submit, reset, or button ;
- Using an <input> element with a type attribute whose value is image;
- Using a <button> element;

Creating Buttons Using the <input> element

When you use the <input> element to create a button, the type of button you create is specified using the type attribute. The type attribute can take the following values to create a button:

- submit, which creates a button that submits a form when pressed
- reset, which creates a button that automatically resets form controls to their initial values as they were when the page loaded
- button, which creates a button that is used to trigger a client-side script when the user clicks that button

Here is an example:

```
<form action="http://www.example.org/feedback.aspx"
method="post">
    <p>
        <input type="submit" name="btnVoteRed"
    value="Vote for reds">
    </p>
    <p>
        <input type="submit" name="btnVoteBlue"
    value="Vote for blues">
```

```
    </p>
    <p>
         <input type="reset" value="Clear form">
    </p>
    <p>
         <input type="button" value="Calculate"
    onclick="calculate()">
    </p>
</form>
```

Creating Buttons Using the <button> element

The <button> element is a more recent introduction that
enables you to specify what appears on a button between an
opening <button> tag and a closing </button> tag so you can
include textual markup or image elements between these tags.
Browsers offer a relief (or 3-D) effect on the button, which
resembles an up or down motion when the button is clicked.
Here is an example:

```
<form action="http://www.example.org/feedback.aspx"
method="post">
    <p>
         <button type="submit">Submit</button>
    </p>
    <p>
         <button type="reset"><b>Clear this form</b>
    I want to start again</button>
    </p>
    <p>
         <button type="button"><img src="submit.gif"
    alt="submit"></button>
    </p>
</form>
```

Check Boxes

Check boxes are like light switches; they can be either on or off. When they are checked, they are on—the user can simply toggle between on and off positions by clicking the check box.

Check boxes can appear individually, with each having its own name, or they can appear as a group of check boxes that share a control name and allow users to select several values for the same property.

Check boxes are ideal form controls when you need to allow a user to:

- Provide a simple yes or no response with one control (such as accepting terms and conditions)

- Select several items from a list of possible options (such as when you want users to indicate all the skills they have from a given list)

A check box is created using the <input> element whose type attribute has a value of checkbox. Following is an example of some check boxes that use the same control name:

```
<form action="http://www.example.com/cv.aspx"
method="get" name="frmCV">
      Which of the following skills do you possess?
Select all that apply.<br>
      <input type="checkbox" name="chkSkills"
value="html">HTML <br>
      <input type="checkbox" name="chkSkills"
value="CSS">CSS<br>
      <input type="checkbox" name="chkSkills"
value="JavaScript">JavaScript<br>
      <input type="checkbox" name="chkSkills"
value="aspnet">ASP.Net<br>
      <input type="checkbox" name="chkSkills"
value="php">PHP
```

```
</form>
```

NOTE For consistency with the naming convention you have used for form elements throughout the chapter, you can start the name of check boxes with the letters chk.

Because all the selected skills will be sent to the processing application in the form of name/value pairs, if someone selects more than one skill, there will be several name/value pairs sent to the server that all share the same name.

Radio Buttons

Radio buttons are similar to check boxes in that they can be either on or off, but there are two key differences:

- When you have a group of radio buttons that share the same name, only one of them can be selected. After one radio button has been selected, if the user clicks another option, the new option is selected and the old one is deselected.

- You should not use radio buttons for a single form control where the control indicates on or off because after a lone radio button has been selected, it cannot be deselected again (without writing a script to do that).

Therefore, a group of radio buttons is ideal if you want to provide users with a number of options from which they must pick only one. In such situations, an alternative is to use a drop-down select box that allows users to select only one option from several. Your decision between whether to use a select box or a group of radio buttons depends on three things:

- **Users' expectations:** If your form models a paper form where users would be presented with several check boxes, from which they can pick only one, then you should use a group of radio buttons.

- **Seeing all the options:** If users would benefit from having all the options in front of them before they pick one, you should use a group of radio buttons.

- **Space:** If you are concerned about space, for example, on a mobile device, a drop-down select box takes up far less space than a set of radio buttons.

NOTE The term "radio buttons" comes from old radios. On some old radios, you could press only one button at a time to select the radio station you wanted to listen to from the ones that had been set. You could not press two of these buttons at the same time on your radio, and pressing one would pop the other out.

The <input> element is again called upon to create radio buttons, and this time the type attribute should be given a value of radio. For example, here radio buttons are used to allow users to select which class of travel they want to take:

```
<form action="http://www.example.com/flights.aspx"
name="frmFlightBooking" method="get">
Please select which class of travel you wish to fly:
<br>
<input type="radio" name="radClass" value="First">First
class <br>
<input type="radio" name="radClass"
value="Business">Business class <br>
<input type="radio" name="radClass"
value="Economy">Economy class <br>
</form>
```

As you can see, the user should be allowed to select only one of the three options, so radio buttons are ideal.

Select Boxes

A drop-down select box enables users to select one item from a drop-down menu. Drop-down select boxes can take up far less space than a group of radio buttons.

Drop-down select boxes can also provide an alternative to single-line text input controls where you want to limit the options that a user can enter. For example, imagine that you were asking which country someone was from. If you had a textbox, visitors from the United States could enter different options such as U.S.A., U.S., United States, America, or North America, whereas with a select box you could control the options they could enter.

A drop-down select box is contained by a <select> element, whereas each individual option within that list is contained within an <option> element. For example, the following form creates a dropdown select box for the user to select a color:

```
<select name="selColor">
      <option selected="selected" value="">Select
      color</option>
      <option value="red">Red</option>
      <option value="green">Green</option>
      <option value="blue">Blue</option>
</select>
```

As you can see here, the text between the opening <option> tags and the closing </option> tags is used to display options to the user, whereas the value that would be sent to the server if that option were selected is given in the value attribute. You can also see that the first <option> element does not have a value and that its content is Select color; this is to indicate to users that they must pick one of the color choices. Finally, notice again the use of the letters sel at the start of the name of a select box.

The width of the select box will be the width of the longest option displayed to the user; in this case, it will be the width of the text Select color. You can update the width of the box using CSS.

The <select> element

The <select> element is the containing element for a drop-down list box.

According to the HTML specification, a <select> element must contain at least one <option> element; although, in practice it should contain more than one <option> element. After all, a drop-down list box with just one option might confuse a user.

The <option> Element

Inside any <select> element, you can find at least one <option> element. The text between the opening <option> and closing </option> tags displays to the user as the label for that option.

Creating Scrolling Select Boxes

As mentioned earlier, you can create scrolling menus where users can see a few of the options in a select box at a time. To do this, you just add the size attribute to the <select> element. The value of the size attribute is the number of options you want to be visible at any one time.

Although scrolling select box menus are rarely used, they can give users an indication that several possible options are open to them and enable them to see a few of the options at the same time. Following is the code for a scrolling select box that enables the user to select a day of the week:

```
<form action="http://www.example.org/days.aspx"
name="frmDays" method="get">
      <select size="4" name="selDay">
            <option value="Mon">Monday</option>
            <option value="Tue">Tuesday</option>
```

```
                <option value="Wed">Wednesday</option>
                <option value="Thu">Thursday</option>
                <option value="Fri">Friday</option>
                <option value="Sat">Saturday</option>
                <option value="Sun">Sunday</option>
        </select> <br><br>
        <input type="submit" value="Submit">
</form>
```

Selecting Multiple Options with the multiple Attribute

The multiple attribute enables users to select more than one item from a select box. When you use this attribute, it is always a good idea to tell people how to select multiple items: by holding down the Control key and clicking the items they want to select.

The addition of this attribute automatically makes the select box look like a scrolling select box. Here you can see an example of a multiple-item select box that enables users to select more than one day of the week:

```
<form action="http://www.example.org/days.aspx"
method="get" name="frmDays">
Please select more than one day of the week (to select
multiple days    hold down the control key and click on
your chosen days):<br>
        <select name="selDays" multiple>
                <option value="Mon">Monday</option>
                <option value="Tue">Tuesday</option>
                <option value="Wed">Wednesday</option>
                <option value="Thu">Thursday</option>
                <option value="Fri">Friday</option>
                <option value="Sat">Saturday</option>
                <option value="Sun">Sunday</option>
        </select> <br><br>
```

```
        <input type="submit" value="Submit">
</form>
```

The result can be seen in a browser.

Grouping Options with the <optgroup> Element

If you have a long list of items in a select box, you can group them together using the <optgroup> element, which acts just like a container element for all the elements you want within a group.

The <optgroup> element must carry a label attribute whose value is a label for that group of options. In the following example, you can see how the options are grouped in terms of type of equipment:

```
<form action="http://www.example.org/info.aspx"
method="get" name="frmInfo">
Please select the product you are interested in:<br>
        <select name="selInformation">
                <optgroup label="Hardware">
                        <option value="Desktop">Desktop
                computers</option>
                        <option value="Laptop">Laptop
                computers</option>    </optgroup>
                <optgroup label="Software">
                        <option value="OfficeSoftware">Office
                software</option>
                        <option value="Games">Games</option>
                </optgroup>
                <optgroup label="Peripherals">
                        <option
                value="Monitors">Monitors</option>
                        <option value="InputDevices">Input
                Devices</option>
                        <option
                value="Storage">Storage</option>
                </optgroup>
```

```
    </select>
    <p><input type="submit" value="Submit"></p>
</form>
```

Different browsers display <optgroup> elements in different ways.

Sending Form Data to the Server

When your browser requests a web page and when the server sends a page back to the browser, you use the HyperText Transfer Protocol (HTTP).

There are two methods that a browser can use to send form data to the server—HTTP get and HTTP post—and you specify which should be used by adding the method attribute on the <form> element.

If the <form> element does not carry a method attribute, then by default the get method will be used. If you use a file upload form control, you must choose the post method. (And you must set the enctype attribute to have a value of multipart/form-data.) Now take a closer look at each of these methods.

HTTP GET

When you send form data to the server using the HTTP get method, the form data is appended to the URL specified in the action attribute of the <form> element.

The form data is separated from the URL using a question mark. Following the question mark, you get the name/value pairs for each form control. Each name/value pair is separated by an ampersand (&).

When a browser requests a URL with any spaces or unsafe characters such as /, \ , =, &, and + (which have special meanings in URLs), they are replaced with a hex code to represent that character. This is done automatically by the browser and is known as URL encoding. When the data reaches the server, the server usually un-encodes the special characters automatically.

One of the advantages of passing form data in a URL is that it can be bookmarked. If you look at searches performed on major search engines such as Google, they tend to use the get method so that the page can be bookmarked.

The get method, however, has some disadvantages. Indeed, when sending sensitive data such as the password shown here, or credit card details, you should not use the get method because the sensitive data becomes part of the URL and is in full view to everyone (and could be bookmarked).

HTTP POST

When you send data from a form to the server using the HTTP post method, the form data is sent transparently in the HTTP headers. Although you do not see these headers, they are not, strictly speaking, secure on their own. If you send sensitive information such as credit card details, the data should be sent under a Secure Sockets Layer (SSL) and should be encrypted.

If the login form you just saw was sent using the post method, it could be represented like this in the HTTP headers:

```
User-agent: MSIE 10 Content-Type: application/x-www-
form-urlencoded Content-length: 35 ...other headers go
here... txtUserName=Bob&pwdPassword=LetMeIn
```

The last line is the form data, which is in exactly the same format as the data after the question mark in the get method—it would also be URL-encoded, so any spaces or unsafe characters such as /, \ , =, &, and + (which have special meanings in URLs) are replaced with a hex code to represent that character as they were in HTTP get requests.

There is nothing to stop you from using the post method to send form data to a page that also contains a query string. For example, you might have one page to handle users who want to subscribe to or unsubscribe from a newsletter, and you might choose to indicate whether users want to subscribe or unsubscribe in the query string. Meanwhile, you might want to send their actual contact details in a form that uses the post method because you are updating a data source.

The only issue with using the HTTP post method is that the information the user entered on the form cannot be bookmarked in the same way it can when it is contained in the URL. So you cannot use it to retrieve a page that was generated using specific form data as you can when you bookmark a page generated by most search engines, but it is good for security reasons.

Summary

This chapter introduced you to the world of creating online forms, which are a vital part of many sites. In most cases, when you want or need to directly collect information from a visitor to your site, you will use a form, and you have seen several examples of forms.

You learned how a form lives inside a <form> element, and that inside a form there are one or more form controls. You know how to use the <input> element to create several kinds of form controls, including many different types of single-line text input controls, as well as check boxes, radio buttons, file upload boxes, buttons, and hidden form controls. You can also use the <textarea> elements to create multiple line text inputs and the <select> and <option> elements to create select boxes. You also learned about new HTML5 elements such as <progress> and <meter> used for marking up complicated UI components simply.

After you create a form with its form controls, you need to ensure that each element is labeled properly so that users know what information they should enter or which selection to make. You can also organize larger forms using the <fieldset> and <label> elements and aid navigation with tabindex and accesskey attributes.

Finally, you learned when you should use the HTTP get or post methods to send form data to the server.

Exercises

Exercise 1

Create an e-mail feedback form. (Example answer provided in back)

- Answers at the end of the book.

Answers

Chapter 1

```
<h1>Ricotta pancake ingredients:</h1>
<ul>
      <li>1 <del>1/2</del><ins>3/4</ins> cups
ricotta</li>
      <li>3/4 cup milk</li>
      <li>4 eggs</li>
      <li>1 cup plain <ins>white</ins> flour</li>
      <li>1 teaspoon baking powder</li>
      <li><del>75g</del><ins>50g</ins> butter</li>
      <li>Pinch of salt</li>
</ul>
```

Chapter 2

Exercise 1

```
<p>The 1<sup>st</sup> time the <b>bold</b> man wrote in
<i>italics</i>, he <em>emphasized</em> several key
words.</p>
```

Exercise 2

menu.html:

```html
<!DOCTYPE html>
<html>
<head>
<meta charset="utf-8">
<title>Example Cafe - Menu</title>
</head>
<body>
     <h1>Example Café</h1>
     <p>Welcome to Example Café. We will be developing
this site    throughout the book.</p>
     <h2>Menu</h2>
     <p>The menu will go here.</p>
</body>
</html>
```

opening.html:

```html
<!DOCTYPE html>
<html>
<head>
<meta charset="utf-8">
<title>Example Cafe - Menu</title>
</head>
<body>
     <h1>Example Café</h1>
     <p>Welcome to Example Café. We will be developing
this site    throughout the book.</p>
     <h2>Opening Hours</h2>
     <p>Details of opening hours and how to find us
will go here. </p>
</body>
</html>
```

contact.html:

```html
<!DOCTYPE html>
<html>
<head>
<meta charset="utf-8">
<title>Example Cafe - Menu</title>
</head>
<body>
     <h1>Example Café</h1>
     <p>Welcome to Example Café. We will be developing
```

```
this site    throughout the book.</p>
      <h2>Contact</h2>
      <p>12 Sea View, Newquay, Cornwall, UK</p>
</body>
</html>
```

Chapter 3

No practice provided

Chapter 4

```
<!DOCTYPE html>
<html>
<head>
<meta charset="utf-8">
<title>Exercise 1</title>
</head>
<body>
      <h1>Icons</h1>
      <p>Here is an icon used to represent a diary.</p>
      <img src="images/diary.gif" alt="Diary"
width="150" height="120" >
      <p>Here is an icon used to represent a
picture.</p>
      <img src="images/picture.gif" alt="Picture"
width="150" height="120" >
      <p>Here is an icon used to represent a news
item.</p>
      <img src="images/news.gif" alt="news" width="150"
height="120" >
</body>
</html>
```

Chapter 5

The <caption> element should appear after the opening <table> element but before the first <tr> element.

Chapter 6

Exercise 1

```
<!DOCTYPE html>
<html>
<head>
<meta charset="utf-8">
<title>Reply to ad</title>
</head>
<body>
    <h1>Reply to ad</h1>
    <p>Use the following form to respond to the
ad:</p>
    <form
action="http://www.example.com/ads/respond.aspx"
method="post" name="frmRespondToAd">
    <table>
        <tr>
            <td><label
        for="emailTo">To</label></td>
            <td><input type="text" name="txtTo"
        readonly="readonly" id="emailTo" size="20"
        value="Star Seller" /></td>
        </tr>
        <tr>
            <td><label
        for="emailFrom">To</label></td>
            <td><input type="text" name="txtFrom"
```

```
                id="emailFrom" size="20" /></td>
            </tr>
            <tr>
                    <td><label
            for="emailSubject">Subject</label></td>
            <td><input type="text" name="txtSubject"
            id="emailSubject"        size="50" /></td>
            </tr>
            <tr>
            <td><label for="emailBody">Body</label></td>
            <td><textarea name="txtBody" id="emailBody"
            cols="50" rows="10"></textarea></td>
            </tr>
        </table>
        <input type="submit" value="Send email" >
        </form>
    </body>
    </html>
```

Conclusion

This book has found you because you have the ultimate potential.

It may be easy to think and feel that you are limited but the truth is you are more than what you have assumed you are. We have been there. We have been in such a situation: when giving up or settling with what is comfortable feels like the best choice. Luckily, the heart which is the dwelling place for passion has told us otherwise.

It was in 2014 when our team was created. Our compass was this – the dream of coming up with books that can spread knowledge and education about programming. The goal was to reach as many people across the world. For them to learn how to program and in the process, find solutions, perform mathematical calculations, show graphics and images, process and store data and much more. Our whole journey to make such dream come true has been very pivotal in our individual lives. We believe that a dream shared becomes a reality.

We want you to be part of this journey, of this wonderful reality. We want to make learning programming easy and fun for you. In addition, we want to open your eyes to the truth that programming can be a start-off point for more beautiful things in your life.

Programming may have this usual stereotype of being too geeky and too stressful. We would like to tell you that nowadays, we enjoy this lifestyle: surf-program-read-write-eat. How amazing is that? If you enjoy this kind of life, we assure you that nothing is impossible and that like us, you can also make programming a stepping stone to unlock your potential to solve problems, maximize solutions, and enjoy the life that you truly deserve.

This book has found you because you are at the brink of everything fantastic!

Thanks for reading!

You can be interested in:

To your success,
Acodemy.

60396004R00074

Made in the USA
Lexington, KY
06 February 2017